THE CHILD DEVELOPMENT ASSOCIATE
ASSESSMENT SYSTEM AND COMPETENCY STANDARDS

Preschool Caregivers in Center-Based Programs

Revised Third Edition

Copies of *Assessment System and Competency Standards for Preschool Caregivers,* Third Edition, are available from:

The Council for Professional Recognition
2460 16th Street, NW
Washington, DC 20009-3547

Visit the Council's Website at http://www.cdacouncil.org.

Photographs courtesy of iStockPhoto.com, BigStockPhoto.com, Morguefile.com, and Ellen Senisi.

Third Edition

First Printing
January 2011

ISBN-10: 0-9820805-1-4
ISBN-13: 978-0-9820805-1-1

Contents

PART III: CDA Competency Standards for Preschool Caregivers in Center-Based Programs

PART IV: Appendices

Preface

The choice to work with 3-, 4-, and 5-year-old children is one of the most important career decisions that one can make. A preschool teacher or caregiver is a special person in children's lives as they master skills, develop friendships, grow in independence, and move to new levels of thinking and understanding about themselves and the world. It is an exciting and challenging responsibility to set up a supportive learning environment for a group of preschoolers, develop a relationship with each one, and meet their needs as individuals and as a group. Children's learning experiences during this period in their lives can increase their self-confidence and readiness for elementary school.

This 2011 third edition includes revisions in the Preschool Competency Standards and the addition of principles for working with dual language learners. The revision process involved reviewing the Competency Standards for their compatibility with current research and knowledge about supporting the healthy development of young children in early childhood centers. Terminology and concepts were updated and then reviewed by panels of experts. Principles for supporting preschoolers who are dual language learners have been added to provide guidance for the growing number of children in early childhood programs whose home language is not English.

The number of 3-, 4-, and 5-year-old children in group programs has multiplied dramatically in recent years. There has been an increase in public school kindergartens, pre-kindergartens, Head Start programs, day care, and many other privately and publicly funded settings. Families place great trust in the staff of these programs, for it is the daily performance of the teacher or caregiver that determines the quality of the children's preschool experience. The Child Development Associate (CDA) Competency Standards and Assessment System support quality programs for preschool children by providing standards for training, evaluation, and recognition of teachers and caregivers based on their ability to meet the unique needs of this age group.

Applying for CDA assessment is a big commitment. However, working towards a CDA Credential can be a rewarding experience. It offers caregivers an opportunity to:

- Take a look at their own work in relation to national standards.

- Get feedback and support from people who have experience working with children and knowledge about early childhood education/child development;

- Improve their skills in ways that are satisfying for themselves and beneficial for children; and

- Earn a professional Credential that is recognized by early childhood educators nationwide.

PART I
The Child Development Associate National Credentialing Program

> *"Becoming a CDA is a process that you work at, learn, and nurture until it grows from within. It is a process by which you grow as an individual and as a professional."*

Overview

The Child Development Associate (CDA) National Credentialing Program is a major national effort initiated in 1971. The purpose of the program is to enhance the quality of child care by defining, evaluating, and recognizing the competence of child care providers and home visitors.

Assessment and credentialing of child care providers is administered by the Council for Professional Recognition (*the* **Council**). More than 260,000 child care providers have earned the CDA Credential since 1975, in all 50 states, the Commonwealth of Puerto Rico, and the U.S. territories of Guam and the Virgin Islands.

The CDA Competency Standards, which define the skills needed by providers in specific child care settings, serve as a means for measuring the overall performance of caregivers during CDA assessment. Assessment is available to caregivers working in several settings — center-based programs serving infants and toddlers, and preschool children; family child care programs; and home visitor programs. An optional bilingual specialization is available to Candidates working in bilingual programs. A CDA Credential is awarded to a person who demonstrates competence in caring for young children by successfully completing the CDA assessment process. Figure 1 illustrates CDA assessment options, and Figure 2 describes the eligible settings for CDA assessment.

Figure 1: Options for CDA Assessment

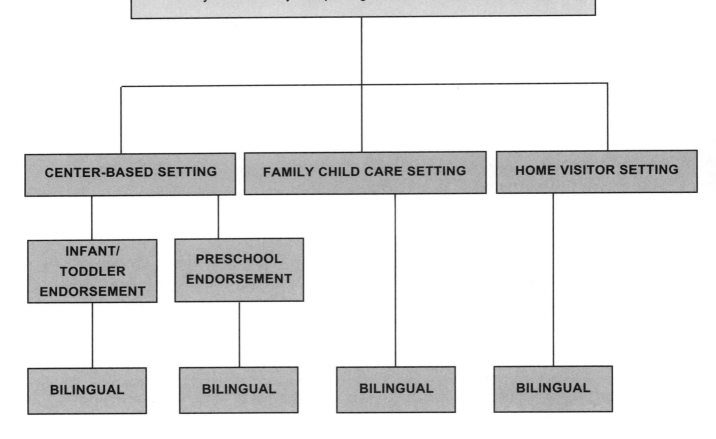

CHILD DEVELOPMENT ASSOCIATE (CDA)

The Child Development Associate, or CDA, is a person who is able to meet the specific needs of children and who, with parents and other adults, works to nurture children's physical, social, emotional, and intellectual growth in a child development framework. The CDA Credential is awarded to child care providers and home visitors who have demonstrated their skill in working with young children and their families by successfully completing the CDA assessment process.

CENTER-BASED SETTING

FAMILY CHILD CARE SETTING

HOME VISITOR SETTING

INFANT/ TODDLER ENDORSEMENT

PRESCHOOL ENDORSEMENT

BILINGUAL

BILINGUAL

BILINGUAL

BILINGUAL

Figure 2: Settings for CDA Assessment

Candidates for the CDA Credential must be observed working in a "setting" that meets the criteria below. (NOTE: Candidates may be employed or work on a volunteer basis in the child care setting):

A center-based preschool setting is a state-approved child development center where a Candidate can be observed working with a group of at least eight children, all of whom are aged 3 through 5 years. In addition, a center-based program must have: (1) at least 10 children enrolled in the program (not necessarily in the Candidate's group), and (2) at least two caregivers working with the children on a regular basis.

A center-based infant/toddler setting is a state-approved child development center where a Candidate can be observed working with a group of at least three children, all of whom are under age 3. In addition, a center-based program must have: (1) at least 10 children enrolled in the program (not necessarily the Candidate's group), and (2) at least two caregivers working with the children on a regular basis.

A family child care setting is a family child care home where a Candidate can be observed working with at least two children 5 years old or younger who are not related to the Candidate by blood or marriage. The setting must meet at least the minimum level of applicable state and/or local regulations. Family child care settings are also eligible in localities where there is no regulation of family child care.

A home visitor setting is an established program of home visits (to families with children 5 years old or younger) that supports parents in meeting the needs of their young children. In this setting, regular home visits are the primary method of program delivery.

A bilingual setting is a child development program that has specific goals for achieving bilingual development in children; where two languages are consistently used in daily activities; and where parents are helped to understand the goals and to support children's bilingual development.

A "Special Education" child development setting — one designed to serve children with moderate to severe special needs — does qualify as an eligible setting for CDA assessment. The CDA Competency Standards address the skills that caregivers need for this population of children. The program must meet the other criteria described above for a preschool, infant/toddler, or family child care setting. The chronological ages of the children with special needs also must match the age groups specified for each setting. All requests for exceptions to the setting requirements must be submitted in writing on a Waiver Request Form (page 35).

The CDA Competency Standards

Candidates for the CDA Credential are assessed based upon the CDA Competency Standards. These national standards are the criteria used to evaluate a caregiver's performance with children and families.

The Competency Standards are divided into **six Competency Goals**, which are statements of a general purpose or goal for caregiver behavior. The six goals are defined in more detail in **13 Functional Areas**, which describe the major tasks or functions that a caregiver must complete to carry out the Competency Goal.

The six Competency Goals are the same for all settings. However, the Functional Area definitions *(and sample behaviors)* differ according to the particular skills needed for specific child care settings and/or age groupings.

Table 1 presents the Competency Goals and Functional Areas for preschool caregiver behavior in center-based settings. The complete CDA Competency Standards for Preschool Caregivers in Center-Based Settings appear in Part III of this book. Each Functional Area has a **developmental context**, which presents a brief overview of relevant child development principles. They also include sample behaviors and examples of caregiver skills.

Table 1: CDA Competency Goals and Functional Areas

CDA COMPETENCY GOALS	FUNCTIONAL AREAS	DEFINITIONS
I. To establish and maintain a safe, healthy learning environment	1. Safe	Candidate provides a safe environment and teaches children safe practices to prevent and reduce injuries.
	2. Healthy	Candidate provides an environment that promotes health and prevents illness, and teaches children about good nutrition and practices that promote wellness.
	3. Learning Environment	Candidate organizes and uses relationships, the physical space, materials, daily schedule, and routines to create a secure, interesting, and enjoyable environment that promotes engagement, play, exploration, and learning of all children including children with disabilities and special needs.
II. To advance physical and intellectual competence	4. Physical	Candidate uses a variety of developmentally appropriate equipment, learning experiences and teaching strategies to promote the physical development (fine motor and gross motor) of all children.
	5. Cognitive	Candidate uses a variety of developmentally appropriate learning experiences and teaching strategies to promote curiosity, reasoning, and problem solving and to lay the foundation for all later learning. Candidate implements curriculum that promotes children's learning of important mathematics, science, technology, social studies and other content goals.
	6. Communication	Candidate uses a variety of developmentally appropriate learning experiences and teaching strategies to promote children's language and early literacy learning, and help them communicate their thoughts and feelings verbally and nonverbally. Candidate helps dual-language learners make progress in understanding and speaking *both* English and their home language.
	7. Creative	Candidate uses a variety of developmentally appropriate learning experiences and teaching strategies for children to explore music, movement, and the visual arts, and to develop and express their individual creative abilities.
III. To support social and emotional development and to provide positive guidance	8. Self	Candidate develops a warm, positive, supportive, and responsive relationship with each child, and helps each child learn about and take pride in his or her individual and cultural identity.
	9. Social	Candidate helps each child function effectively in the group, learn to express feelings, acquire social skills, and make friends, and promotes mutual respect among children and adults.
	10. Guidance	Candidate provides a supportive environment and uses effective strategies to promote children's self-regulation and support acceptable behaviors, and effectively intervenes for children with persistent challenging behaviors.
IV. To establish positive and productive relationships with families	11. Families	Candidate establishes a positive, responsive, and cooperative relationship with each child's family, engages in two-way communication with families, encourages their involvement in the program, and supports the child's relationship with his or her family.
V. To ensure a well-run, purposeful program that is responsive to participant needs	12. Program Management	Candidate is a manager who uses observation, documentation, and planning to support children's development and learning and to ensure effective operation of the classroom or group. The Candidate is a competent organizer, planner, record keeper, communicator, and a cooperative co-worker.
VI. To maintain a commitment to professionalism	13. Professionalism	Candidate makes decisions based on knowledge of research-based early childhood practices, promotes high-quality in child care services, and takes advantage of opportunities to improve knowledge and competence, both for personal and professional growth and for the benefit of children and families.

The CDA Assessment System: Direct Route

A CDA assessment is the process by which a caregiver's competence is evaluated by the Council for Professional Recognition (the Council). In preparation for assessment, the Candidate documents her/his skill in relation to the CDA Competency Standards. Five components make up the documentation:

1. The Professional Resource File
2. The Parent Opinion Questionnaires
3. The CDA Assessment Observation Instrument
4. The Early Childhood Studies Review
5. The Oral Interview

The results are submitted to the Council for review by a committee, which makes the decision whether to award the CDA Credential to the Candidate.

A. Stages of Assessment

There are six stages in the CDA Assessment system: (1) Inquiry; (2) Collection of Documentation by the Candidate; (3) Application; (4) Verification Visit by the Council Representative; (5) Credential Award; and (6) Credential Renewal. These stages are summarized here and explained in detail in Part II of this book.

1. Inquiry

Individuals who meet all the Candidate eligibility requirements in Part II of this book and who can be observed in an eligible setting should purchase a packet of application materials from the Council. The packet contains all the instructions and forms necessary for the next stages of assessment.

2. Collection of Documentation by the Candidate

The Candidate chooses an early childhood professional — an Advisor — who conducts a formal observation, using the CDA Assessment Observation Instrument.

The Candidate distributes and collects Parent Opinion Questionnaires to determine parents' opinion of her or his work with children.

The Candidate also prepares a Professional Resource File which contains an autobiographical statement, written examples of her or his competence in each of the six CDA Competency Areas, and a collection of resource materials.

3. Application

When the collection of documentation is complete, the Candidate, Advisor, and the Program Director sign the Direct Assessment Application Form, which the Candidate sends to the Council with the assessment fee and training documentation.

4. Verification Visit by the Council Representative

The Council assigns a specially trained early childhood professional to administer a written examination of knowledge of good practices — the Early Childhood Studies Review. This person will conduct an oral interview with the Candidate and check the Professional Resource File, the CDA Assessment Observation Instrument, and the Parent Opinion Questionnaires.

At the conclusion of the Verification Visit, the Council Representative will send the results to the Council in Washington, DC.

5. Credential Award

A committee of the Council conducts a review of the Candidate's documentation of competence and makes a decision regarding credential award. If a Credential is awarded, the official Credential is sent to the new Child Development Associate. If the committee decides the Candidate needs more training, the Council notifies the Candidate and informs her/him of appeal procedures and other subsequent options.

6. Credential Renewal

A CDA Credential is valid for three years from the date of award, after which it may be renewed for five-year periods. CDAs may renew their Credential only for the original setting, age-level endorsement, and specialization.

Confidentiality Statement

All communication about CDA Candidates is confidential. The Council will not release assessment information without the Candidate's permission.

B. Pacing the Assessment

The Council accepts Direct Assessment Applications on a rolling basis. Your Verification Visit will occur within 90 days from the date the Council receives your <u>complete and correct</u> Application. To avoid any delays, we encourage you to use the Candidate Checklist located on page 34 to ensure your Application is filled out correctly and the documents you prepared meet Council requirements.

"Becoming a CDA is not a faraway dream
that you can't touch;
rather, it is a process that is
well within the grasp of reality."

PART II

Eligibility and Documentation Requirements for Center-Based Preschool Assessments

The eligibility and documentation requirements that follow ensure that the Candidate has training and experience, and that accurate information about the Candidate's performance as a primary caregiver will be gathered during the assessment process. The Council will use the information to evaluate the Candidate's ability to meet the needs of preschool children in a child development framework.

Candidate Eligibility Requirements

The applicant must meet the following eligibility requirements and submit records as instructed on the Direct Assessment Application Form:

A. Personal

1. Hold a High School diploma or equivalent, or be enrolled as a junior or senior in a high school vocational program in early education.

2. Be able to speak, read, and write well enough to fulfill the responsibilities of a CDA Candidate.

3. Sign a statement of ethical conduct.

B. Setting

Identify a state-approved child development center where the Candidate can be observed *working as **lead caregiver*** with a group of at least eight children, who are aged 3 to 5 years. In addition, a center-based program must have:

1. at least 10 children enrolled in the program *(not necessarily the Candidate's group)*; **and**

2. at least two caregivers who work with the children on a regular basis.

> *"I have watched the growth of some of the past CDA Candidates. Their confidence and work with young children has improved tremendously since receiving their Credentials. The end result is a competent child care professional."*
>
> —Mary Graves
> CDA Instructor

Center-based programs include a wide variety of schedules, services, purposes, funding sources, and educational methods. Nursery school, preschool, kindergarten, child development program, day care, Head Start, lab school, and parent co-op are other names for programs that may meet the CDA requirements for a center-based setting. They may operate a few hours a day, a few days a week, or all day, five days a week. The daily schedule can also be a structured or unstructured one. Child care programs can also be in churches, public schools, universities, or privately owned facilities. Financing for these programs can be through parents, industry, federal government, or state government. The program can also be for-profit or nonprofit.

The staff in a center-based program may be trained to implement specific curricula, and second language learning may be integrated into daily activities. Religious training may be emphasized, or the program may combine philosophies, methods, and materials from many different sources.

C. Experience

Candidates must have had, within the past five years, at least 480 hours of experience working with children aged 3 through 5 in a group setting.

D. Education

Candidates must have completed, within the past five years, 120 clock hours of formal child care education, with no fewer than 10 hours in each of the following eight subject areas. This requirement may be met through participation in the wide variety of training available in the field, including in-service. **Training obtained at conferences or from individual consultants is not acceptable.**

Table 2: Education Requirements for CDA Preschool Candidates

Subject Areas	Examples
1. **Planning a safe and healthy learning environment**	Safety, first aid, health, nutrition, space planning, materials and equipment, play
2. **Advancing children's physical and intellectual development**	Large and small muscle, language and literacy, discovery, art, music, mathematics, social studies, science, technology, and dual language learning
3. **Supporting children's social and emotional development**	Adult modeling, self-esteem, self-regulation, socialization, cultural identity, conflict resolution
4. **Building productive relationships with families**	Parent involvement, home visits, conferences, referrals, communication strategies
5. **Managing an effective program operation**	Planning, record keeping, reporting, community services
6. **Maintaining a commitment to professionalism**	Advocacy, ethical practices, work force issues, professional development, goal setting, networking
7. **Observing and recording children's behavior**	Tools and strategies for objective observation and assessment of children's behavior and learning to plan curriculum and individualize teaching, developmental delays, intervention strategies, individual education plans
8. **Understanding principles of child development and learning**	Typical developmental expectations for children from birth through age 5, individual variation including children with special needs, cultural influences on development

All the formal education hours must be under the auspices of an agency or organization with expertise in early childhood teacher preparation. The education could be for college credit or for no credit.

Such agencies and organizations include, but are not limited to:

- Four-year colleges and universities

- Two-year junior and community colleges

- Vocational and technical schools

- Early childhood education/child care programs that sponsor training, such as Head Start, U.S. Army Child and Youth Services, or school districts

- Divisions of state or federal governments, or branches of the U.S. Military Services

- Resource and referral agencies

Candidates may accumulate the hours from a single training program (not an individual consultant), or from a combination of programs. Each agency or organization must provide verification of the Candidate's education in the form of a transcript, certificate, or letter. It is the Candidate's responsibility to supplement the verification by citing the number of clock hours completed in each required area of study on the Direct Assessment Application Form.

E. Bilingual Specialization

In addition to the requirements above, Candidates for bilingual specialization must: (1) work in a bilingual program that requires the Candidate to speak both languages daily and consistently; and (2) have a working knowledge of two languages.

A working knowledge of two languages means the ability to speak, read, and write well enough to understand others and to be understood by others. In Bilingual Specialization Assessments, one of the skills being assessed is the Candidate's ability to consistently use both languages in daily activities.

There is no one model of bilingual education that a Candidate for the CDA bilingual specialization should follow. A competent Candidate is knowledgeable about the development of language, bilingual communication, and the integration of culture and language. The bilingual program setting should have specific program goals for achieving bilingual development, and Candidates should implement them through consistent, daily opportunities for children to build on their first language and culture and to learn the second language. This can include programs where children who speak English are learning a second language.

A Candidate for Bilingual Specialization must meet specific documentation requirements and must select an Advisor who meets Bilingual Requirements *(see page XX78)*. *A Candidate who wants to complete assessment using a language combination other than English/Spanish must contact the Council for guidance.*

F. Monolingual Assessments

Under special circumstances, Candidates may request a monolingual assessment in Spanish or another language. These are Candidates who work as primary caregivers with a group of children where they serve as the role model for a language other than English, and consistently conduct daily activities using this language.

Individuals whose work requires them to use a language other than Spanish or English, and who wish to be assessed in that language, must contact the Council for further guidelines. The language of the assessment is determined by the language that the program requires a Candidate to use.

G. Overseas Assessments

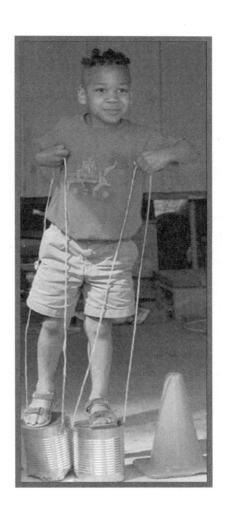

The Council only conducts CDA assessments in the United States and Puerto Rico, except by special arrangements with the U.S. Army Child Development Services. If Candidates outside the United States or Puerto Rico want to obtain the CDA Credential, they must contact the Council to discuss the procedures and additional expenses.

H. Waivers

The Council will consider waiving certain eligibility requirements if an individual provides a written explanation for the request. All such requests should be sent directly to the Council BEFORE submitting an application. After reviewing the waiver request, the individual will be notified whether it has been granted. Waiver petitions must be documented on the Waiver Request Form at the end of Part II of this manual.

Candidate Documentation Requirements

The Candidate must present evidence of her/his competence through written documentation. Five components make up the documentation:

1. The Professional Resource File
    prepared by the Candidate

2. The Parent Opinion Questionnaires
    collected by the Candidate

3. The CDA Assessment Observation Instrument
    completed by the Advisor

4. The Early Childhood Studies Review
    administered by the Council Rep

5. The Oral Interview
    conducted by the Council Rep

The documentation evidence is organized in two sections. First, the Candidate presents evidence of his or her competence from the following three sources:

1. The Professional Resource File

2. The Parent Opinion Questionnaires

3. The CDA Assessment Observation Instrument completed by the Advisor

Next, the Candidate completes the Early Childhood Studies Review and the Oral Interview during the Council Rep's Verification Visit.

A. Professional Resource File

The Professional Resource File is a collection of materials that early childhood professionals use in their work with young children and their families. Compiling the Resource File has two purposes:

1. It provides a picture of what information Candidates find valuable in their work (as a basis for assessing competence as a CDA); and

2. It provides Candidates an important experience in locating resources and articulating their own view of the work in early childhood programs.

The Professional Resource File is a working resource — one that should be **useful** to a CDA during her/his career in early childhood education. The information it contains should serve as daily reference material.

Arrangement of the Resource File

The material in the Professional Resource File can be arranged in any one of many creative ways *(for example, bound in a notebook or contained inside folders in a file box)*. It should be professional looking, manageable in size, and legible. It should be easy to add to or delete from. *There are no requirements about **how** it should look.* Whatever its physical form, the Professional Resource File should be portable. It should be designed to be carried to and from a work site, on a home visit, or to a meeting.

Contents

The Professional Resource File has three major sections: (1) Autobiography; (2) Statements of Competence; and (3) Resource Collection. Below is an explanation of what CDA Candidates must do to prepare the Resource File.

1. Autobiography

The Candidate writes a statement about her/himself of about 300 words. In the first part, the Candidate tells who s/he is, and in the second part, tells what things about her/his life influenced the decision to work with young children. *If the Candidate wishes, s/he may attach a formal resume of education and work experiences.* For Bilingual Candidates, the autobiography may be written in either language.

2. Statements of Competence

The Candidate writes six statements of competence based on the following six Competency Goals. **The Candidate begins each section by writing out the following Competency Goal Statement:**

Goal 1. To establish and maintain a safe, healthy learning environment

Goal 2. To advance physical and intellectual competence

Goal 3. To support social and emotional development and to provide positive guidance

Goal 4. To establish positive and productive relationships with families

Goal 5. To ensure a well-run, purposeful program responsive to participant needs

Goal 6. To maintain a commitment to professionalism

In the Candidate's own words, s/he describes the things s/he does with children and families. The description should demonstrate the Candidate's ability to meet the specific needs of children and families in each of the six CDA Competency Goals and 13 Functional Areas. The description in each statement of competence should be 200–500 words in length and should state the Candidate's goals or objectives for children and give specific examples of what s/he does with the children *(activities)* to achieve those goals. *For Bilingual Candidates, all statements must be specific to the goals of bilingual programs and reflect the Candidate's bilingual work with children and families. The statements in three Competency Goal areas must be written in Spanish or other language.*

Remember, each statement of competence should contain no more than 500 words. While the Candidate cannot describe everything s/he does in such a limited space, s/he should choose the most important goals for children and the best examples of practices that represent her/his competence. **The examples listed in Part III of this book are samples provided for reference and are not to be copied or reworded.**

The Candidate is to write about *current practice,* using examples of her/his work within the past six months *(the six months before the time s/he submits the Direct Assessment Application Form).*

3. *Resource Collection*

The third part of the Professional Resource File consists of 17 specific items called the Resource Collection. They should be organized by Competency Goal areas and numbered so that each item can be located easily during the Council Representative verification visit. *Do not mix them with your statements of competence. For Candidates applying for the **Bilingual Specialization**, the resources used directly with children and families must be in two languages (English and another language). These are items 4, 5, 6, 7, 8, 10, 11, 12, 15, and 16. For **Monolingual** (other than English) Candidates, items 4, 5, 6, 7, 8, 10, 11, 12, 15, and 16 must be in the other language.*

COMPETENCY GOAL I

To establish and maintain a safe, healthy learning environment

1. Provide a summary of the legal requirements in your state regarding child abuse and neglect (including contact information for the appropriate agency), and also your program's policy regarding your responsibility to report child abuse and neglect.

2. Include the current certificate of completion of a certified pediatric first-aid training course (that includes treatment for blocked airway and providing rescue breathing for infants and young children). Certification must have been within the past three years.

3. Use the Internet, public library, or your program's professional library to obtain the name and contact information for an agency that supplies information on nutrition for children and/or nutrition education for families (for example, *Cooperative Extension Service or Child Care Food Program*).

4. Provide a sample of your weekly plan that includes goals for children's learning and development, brief description of planned learning experiences, and also accommodations for children with special needs (whether for children you currently serve or may serve in the future).

COMPETENCY GOAL II

To advance physical and intellectual competence

5. Select four songs, fingerplays, word games, or poems that you can use to promote phonological awareness. Describe strategies to promote phonological awareness among children whose home language is other than English.

6. Describe nine learning experiences for 3-, 4-, and 5-year-old children (three for 3-year-olds, three for 4-year-olds, and three for 5-year-olds). Each learning experience should promote physical, cognitive, and creative development. Describe the goals, materials, and teaching strategies used.

COMPETENCY GOAL III

To support social and emotional development and to provide positive guidance

7. Provide the titles, authors, publishers, copyright dates, and a short summary for each of ten age-appropriate children's books **that you use** to support development of children's self-concept and self-esteem, and to help children deal with life's challenges. These books may support development of cultural and linguistic group identity; gender identity; children with disabilities or special needs; separation, divorce, remarriage, or blended families; everyday activities and routines; and/or the cycle of life from human reproduction to death.

8. Use the Internet, public library, or your program's professional library to obtain at least two resources designed to assist teachers in constructively dealing with children with challenging behaviors (such as aggressive behavior like hitting or biting, or shyness).

9. Provide the name and telephone number of an agency in the community where you work for making referrals to family counseling.

COMPETENCY GOAL IV

To establish positive and productive relationships with families

10. Find out where to obtain resources, materials, and translation services for families whose home language is other than English. Provide the agency name and contact information.

11. Document your program's policies that specify parents' responsibilities and what the program does for parents.

COMPETENCY GOAL V

To ensure a well-run, purposeful program responsive to participant needs

12. Provide three samples of recordkeeping forms used in early childhood programs. Include an accident report, emergency form, and a third form of your choice.

COMPETENCY GOAL VI

To maintain a commitment to professionalism

13. Use the Internet, public library, or your program's professional library to obtain the name, address, and phone number of your state's agency that regulates child care centers and homes. These regulations are available electronically at the website of the National Resource Center for Health and Safety in Child Care (http://nrckids.org/STATES/states.htm). Make a copy of the section(s) that describes qualification requirements for personnel (teachers, directors, and assistants). Describe two important requirements related to your job responsibilities.

14. Review the websites of two or three national early childhood associations (one with a local affiliate) to obtain information about membership, their resources, and how to order (if necessary, use the public library for Internet access). Download at least two resources from the Internet that will enhance your work.

15. Obtain four pamphlet(s) or articles (may be downloaded from the Internet) designed to help parents understand how young children develop and learn.

    Articles must help parents understand development and learning of 3- to 5-year-olds. At least one article must relate to guidance.

16. Locate an observation tool to use in recording information about children's behavior. One copy should be blank; the other one should be filled out as a sample of your observation of an individual child. *(The child's name should not be included.)*

17. Obtain contact information for at least two agencies in the community that provide resources and services for children with disabilities (in most communities, the local school district provides these services).

B. Parent Opinion Questionnaires

Parent perceptions about a Candidate's skills and knowledge are extremely important in the CDA assessment. Each parent with a child in the Candidate's care will complete a questionnaire. **The information that the parents provide is confidential. No one is allowed to read the parent responses (this includes the Candidate), except authorized Council Officials.**

The Parent Opinion Questionnaire is in the application packet. The Candidate prepares to distribute the questionnaires by filling out the information on the cover letter, including name, the date s/he expects the questionnaire to be returned, and telephone number. The Candidate should speak to each parent by telephone or in person. Each family is to receive only one questionnaire. The Candidate should briefly explain about the CDA assessment, the parents' participation, the questionnaires, and why s/he wants to obtain a CDA Credential. S/he should emphasize how important it is for each of them to fill out and promptly return their questionnaire.

Here are some ideas about how to distribute the questionnaires. The Candidate may use any combination of the methods listed below:

Group Meeting: Include a CDA/parent questionnaire presentation as part of the agenda of a meeting already scheduled, or call for a special meeting. This will allow the Candidate to discuss and answer questions — in person — from parents about the Credentialing process and the role of the parents.

Mailing: Some Candidates prefer mailing questionnaires to parents. If the Candidate chooses to do this, it is a good idea to enclose a self-addressed, stamped envelope. Then the Candidate should follow up with a courtesy telephone call.

Individual Help: Some parents may require extra help. The Candidate may ask someone in the program to assist parents who are having difficulty understanding the questions. Because the questionnaires are confidential, the Candidate may not get involved at this level. If there are parents with special needs, please call the Council for advice. We will be happy to provide assistance.

There may also be parents who speak a language other than English or Spanish. Do not overlook these parents. If necessary, the Candidate should find someone who can translate the questions to the parent *(either in writing, or orally)*.

Each questionnaire **is to be returned to the Candidate in a sealed envelope.** The Candidate must collect all the envelopes and place them in a larger sealed envelope, with both the number distributed and the number returned recorded on the outside of the envelope. Remember, the goal is to collect at least 75% of all parent questionnaires distributed.

"Earning the CDA Credential gives CDAs a sense of pride, increases their self-esteem, and instills confidence."

C. Formal Observation

A vital source of evidence of a Candidate's skill is actual hands-on work as primary caregiver with children and families. Documentation of these practices is collected through formal observation conducted by an Advisor (see following section).

Advisor Information

A. Identifying an Advisor

The Candidate must identify an early childhood professional who is willing to serve as Advisor *and* who meets the Advisor qualifications that appear in Appendix C. For example, Candidates may select a Program Director, a trainer, an Education Coordinator, a site supervisor, or a college instructor. The Council operates a national Advisor Registry. The Council can provide the names of qualified Advisors for Candidates who need assistance in locating an eligible early childhood professional.

B. The Role of the Advisor

The Advisor observes the Candidate *while working as **lead teacher** with young children in an eligible setting*, and records the Candidate's consistent performance using the *CDA Assessment Observation Instrument*. To complete the instrument and prepare the final ratings in all 13 Functional Areas may take one visit or several visits. More detailed instructions for completing the instrument are located in the CDA Assessment Observation Instrument book.

C. Number of Observations

The Candidate will arrange a time with the Advisor to conduct one or more observations, but the Advisor should conduct and date the observation within six months before the Candidate submits the Direct Assessment Application to the Council. Each observation should take a minimum of $2\,^1/_2$–3 hours.

D. Confidentiality

The Advisor must not share or give feedback to anyone (including the Candidate) and, when completed, should place the instrument in a sealed envelope before giving it to the Candidate. The Candidate keeps the sealed envelope and takes it to the Verification Visit.

E. Special Requirements

For Bilingual Candidates, the Advisor may use the Spanish or English CDA Observation Instrument, and may complete it in either language or a combination of both languages. However, the information provided must reflect the bilingual work of the Candidate with children and families, and the Candidate's ability to consistently use both languages on a daily basis.

For monolingual (Spanish) Candidates, the Advisor must use the Spanish Assessment Observation Instrument and all information must be written only in Spanish.

A Message to Advisors

As a professional in the field of early childhood education/child development, you have the experience and knowledge that will help a person who has chosen to care for children. You can support her/his development in cooperation with parents and other early childhood professionals. The information you collect about the Candidate's work will make a major contribution towards his/her evaluation of competence. We know that the time and effort required to complete your responsibilities as a CDA Advisor is significant. Your contribution is tremendously important to our national effort to assure quality child care for young children.

Serving as Advisor does not require you to "train" the Candidate in the CDA Competency Areas, although many Advisors do serve as trainers. The Advisor's role, as required by the Council, is to document evidence of the Candidate's consistent performance during the observation(s), using the CDA Assessment Observation Instrument.

F. Candidate Performance Items To Be Rated on the Observation Instrument

The purpose of the observation at the Candidate's worksite is to rate a Candidate's skill in specific performance areas.

Functional Area 1: Safe

1.1 All toys and materials provided for use by children are safe.
1.2 Supervision is appropriate for developmental level of children.
1.3 Emergency procedures are planned in advance and are well organized.

Functional Area 2: Healthy

2.1 General hygiene practices are consistently implemented to cut down the spread of infectious disease.
2.2 Health maintenance habits in children are encouraged.
2.3 Diapering/toileting procedures are organized to maintain health.
2.4 Meals/snacks meet the developmental needs of children.
2.5 Pleasant and appropriate environment conducive to rest is provided daily.

Functional Area 3: Learning Environment

3.1 Well-arranged space, which meets the developmental needs of children during routines and play is provided.
3.2 A variety of developmentally-appropriate materials are available.
3.3 Materials for play are well organized.
3.4 Schedule provided meets the children's need for routine and play.

Functional Area 4: Physical

4.1 A variety of activities are offered which enable children to develop their large muscles.
4.2 A variety of activities are offered which enable children to develop their small muscles.
4.3 Program activities adapt to meet individual needs and special needs of children with disabilities.
4.4 Opportunities are offered to help children develop their senses.

Functional Area 5: Cognitive

5.1 A variety of age-appropriate materials and activities that encourage curiosity, exploration, and problem-solving are accessible to children throughout the day.

5.2 Interactions provide support for play, exploration, and learning.

5.3 Individual learning styles are recognized.

Functional Area 6: Communication

6.1 Communication with each child is frequent.

6.2 Talk with children is developmentally appropriate.

6.3 Children are encouraged to talk.

6.4 Children's attempts to communicate are responded to positively.

6.5 A developmentally-appropriate, print-rich environment, in which children learn about books, literature, and writing, is provided.

Functional Area 7: Creative

7.1 Individual expression and creativity are appreciated.

7.2 Many appropriate music experiences are available to children.

7.3 Art experiences are age appropriate and varied.

7.4 Dramatic play experiences, with a variety of age-appropriate props, are available.

7.5 A variety of age-appropriate block play opportunities are available.

Functional Area 8: Self

8.1 Children are given the message that each is important, respected, and valued.

8.2 Individual children are able to develop a sense of security.

8.3 Diapering/toileting procedures are developmentally appropriate and set up to encourage self-help skills.

Functional Area 9: Social

9.1 Each child feels accepted in the group.

9.2 Feelings of empathy and respect for others are encouraged.

9.3 Non-biased curriculum is used.

9.4 Children are encouraged to respect the environment.

Functional Area 10: Guidance

10.1 Methods for avoiding problems are implemented.

10.2 Positive guidance techniques are used.

10.3 Guidance practices are related to knowledge of each child's personality and developmental level.

Functional Area 11: Families

11.1 Various opportunities to appreciate children's families are part of the regular program.

11.2 Information about families' culture, religion, and childrearing practices is in classroom experiences.

11.3 Various opportunities are offered to help parents understand the development of their child and understand their child's point of view.

11.4 Resources are provided to help families meet their child's needs.

In addition, the Advisor will rate the Candidate's performance in the two additional CDA Functional Areas where it may not be possible to observe behavior during the formal observation. The Advisor may need to ask the Candidate some questions to complete her/his evidence in the following areas:

Functional Area 12: Program Management

Candidate manages, by using all available resources, to ensure an effective operation. Candidate is a competent organizer, planner, recordkeeper, communicator, and a cooperative coworker.

Functional Area 13: Professionalism

Candidate makes decisions based on knowledge of early childhood theories and practices, and promotes quality child care services. The Candidate also takes advantage of opportunities to improve competence, both for personal and professional growth and for the benefit of children and families.

Candidate keeps abreast of current regulatory, legislative and workforce issues and how they affect the welfare of young children.

The Direct Assessment Application Form

A Candidate is ready to apply for Direct Assessment when all eligibility requirements have been met — Personal, Setting, Education, and Documentation, as outlined on pages 9–21.

The Direct Assessment Application Form is the official Candidate application for CDA Assessment. Instructions for completing it are on the form. Space is provided for the Candidate and the Advisor to verify all eligibility and documentation collection requirements. The application also requires consent from the Program Director for the Candidate to participate in the Verification Visit.

The Candidate then submits the application with the assessment fee and original signatures. *Faxes or photocopies are unacceptable.*

The Verification Visit

When the Council receives the Application Form, the fee, and all training verification, a Council Rep will be selected to conduct the Verification Visit. The Rep will contact the Candidate to make arrangements for the date and place for the Visit.

Before the Council Representative arrives, Candidates should prepare all documentation by doing the following:

1. Check to see that all entries in the Professional Resource File are complete. *Make a copy of the "Autobiography" and "Statements of Competence."* The Council Rep will return the File to the Candidate, and mail the copied autobiography and statements to the Council. The 17 items will remain with the Candidate.

2. Obtain the completed *CDA Assessment Observation Instrument* from the Advisor. Both forms should be in a sealed envelope for the Council Rep to mail to the Council.

3. Obtain the completed Parent Opinion Questionnaires. They must also be in sealed envelopes for the Council Rep to mail to the Council.

During the Verification Visit, the Council Rep will check that the following items are present:

1. The "Autobiography" and "Statements of Competence" in the Professional Resource File.

2. The 17 Resource Collection items in the Professional Resource File.

3. The Parent Opinion Questionnaires.

4. The CDA Assessment Observation Instrument.

In addition, the Council Rep will:

5. Administer the Early Childhood Studies Review.

6. Conduct the Oral Interview.

A. Early Childhood Studies Review

The arrangements for taking the Early Childhood Studies Review will be discussed when the Council Rep contacts the Candidate. In addition, the Candidate will be asked to arrange a private place for the Council Rep to review documents, to conduct the Oral Interview, and to administer the Early Childhood Studies Review. It is preferable to use space at the Center where you work. *Permission must first be obtained from the Program Director.*

The Early Childhood Studies Review is a written examination designed to measure general knowledge of good practices in early childhood education programs serving children aged from birth through age 5. The content of the Review is based on those current principles of developmentally appropriate practice widely accepted among early childhood professionals.

Bilingual Candidates will take the Early Childhood Studies Review in English.

The Early Childhood Studies Review takes approximately two hours to complete and contains 60 questions, like the examples below. Each question has four answers to choose from. The following have been marked to show the correct answer:

What is the best age to introduce music to children?

- ● a. Infants
- ○ b. Toddlers
- ○ c. Young preschoolers
- ○ d. Older preschoolers

To keep children from interrupting activities in busy places, what is the most appropriate thing to do?

- ● a. Use furniture to make clear pathways that go around spaces.
- ○ b. Have children choose one place to play until playtime is over.
- ○ c. Teach the rule, "We walk through other children's play spaces carefully and quietly."
- ○ d. Have children do most of their play on tables.

Which is the most nutritious snack for toddlers?

- ○ a. Cookies and milk
- ○ b. Corn chips and 100% fruit juice
- ● c. Apple slices, graham crackers, and milk
- ○ d. Saltine crackers and 100% fruit juice

The Early Childhood Studies Review may be administered orally. However, if the Candidate wishes to use this option, arrangements must be made in advance. There will be an additional cost for this service.

While the Candidate is taking the written examination, the Council Rep will review the Candidate's documentation. Following the review, the Council Rep will conduct the Oral Interview.

B. Oral Interview

The Oral Interview provides an opportunity for Candidates to show how the knowledge they have acquired through experience and training would be applied in a variety of early childhood settings.

The interview consists of 10 structured situations and takes about one and a half hours to administer. The situations are specific to the Candidate's setting, age-level endorsement and specialization.

For each situation, the Council Rep will show the Candidate a picture with a written description of the activity pictured. The Council Rep will read aloud the description as the Candidate reads along. Then s/he will pose a question and ask the Candidate to respond. The Council Rep will listen, make notes and identify various aspects of the response. S/he may ask additional questions to help the Candidate give a clear and complete response.

Bilingual Candidates must select the language they will use for their Oral Interview and must indicate their preference on the Direct Assessment Application.

A sample interview question follows:

SAMPLE INTERVIEW QUESTION

The adult in charge of a group of 16 3-year-olds believes that mealtime should be a time for relaxing and learning. There are two tables for the children and one table for the adults.

After the adult sets the table and serves each child's plate, mealtime begins. He makes sure that children sit still at the table, and because he wants them to learn good habits, they are not allowed to eat with their hands or make noises. They all begin eating at the same time and may be excused from the table only when everyone has finished. Then, all together, they brush their teeth in the bathroom as a group activity.

What do you think of this situation?

When the interview is finished, the Council Rep will score the responses.

C. Concluding the Verification Visit

At the conclusion of the Verification Visit, *the Council Rep will return the following documents to the Candidate:*

1. The original Autobiography

2. The original Statements of Competence

3. The 17-item Resource Collection from the Professional Resource File

The Council Rep will send the following materials to the Council:

1. A copy of the Autobiography
2. A copy of the Statements of Competence
3. The CDA Assessment Observation Instrument and Supplemental Observation Form
4. The Parent Opinion Questionnaires
5. The Early Childhood Studies Review
6. The Oral Interview booklet

Once the Council receives the above documentation, a committee will review the materials and make a final decision. If the Credential is awarded, the official Credential is sent to the new Child Development Associate. If the committee decides the Candidate needs more training, the Council will notify the Candidate and inform her/him of appeal procedures and other subsequent options.

Renewal Procedures

A CDA Credential is valid for three years from the date of award, after which it may be renewed for five-year periods. CDAs may renew their Credential only for the original setting, age-level endorsement, and specialization.

Under the renewal procedures, all CDA Renewal Candidates must do the following:

- Document proof of a **current Red Cross or other agency First Aid Certificate**.

- Document proof of at least **4.5 Continuing Education Units (CEUs), or a three-credit-hour course in early childhood education/child development**. These hours must be in addition to the original 120 clock hours or three formal or informal educational experiences required when the Candidate obtained the CDA Credential. Bilingual CDAs must meet this requirement with coursework incorporating bilingual issues.

- Document proof of **recent (within current year) work experience with young children (a minimum of 80 hours)**.

- **Select an Early Childhood Education professional who must complete a Letter of Recommendation Form regarding the CDA's competence with young children.**

- Document proof (within current year) of **membership in a national or local early childhood professional organization**.

Second Setting CDA Credential

For CDAs who hold one Credential and wish to obtain a second CDA Credential in a different setting, we offer the Second Setting CDA Credential. The Second Setting CDA is available to center-based and family child care CDAs who received their Credentials under the revised direct assessment procedures on or after January 1, 1993. CDAs who received their Credentials under the Local Assessment Team (LAT) procedures may apply for a second Credential by completing the revised Direct Assessment process.

The choice to work with young children and their families is one of the most important career decisions that one can make in our society. Best wishes for a rewarding and successful career!

Help Desk Information

A. Contact the Council

The Council maintains a toll-free hotline to answer questions and to provide assistance. Call **800-424-4310** (toll-free) or **202-265-9090** between 9:00 A.M. and 5:00 P.M. Eastern Standard Time.

B. Commonly Asked Questions About Direct Assessment

Q. **What is the fee?**

The fee for direct assessment changes from time to time. The current fee is on the Direct Assessment Application Form.

Q. **Where can I find a CDA training program?**

Inquire at a local postsecondary education institution — vocational school, college or university. Early childhood education, child development and home economics programs offer coursework and field supervision that will help Candidates acquire the skills needed for CDA assessment. The Council also offers CDA training through the CDA Professional Preparation Program (CDA P_3). This program involves one year of structured study. Contact the Council for more information.

Q. **Is financial assistance available to help pay the assessment fee?**

The CDA Scholarship Program, funded by the federal government, has been discontinued. However, some state and local organizations continue to offer financial assistance for training, and in some cases, for assessment fees for CDA Candidates. Inquire through your employer or your local early childhood education professional association. In addition, in most communities, low- to no-cost training is provided by resource and referral agencies.

Q. **Does employer-sponsored in-service training count toward the 120 clock hours of formal education?**

Yes, as long as the agency has expertise in early childhood teacher preparation.

Q. **Can I be assessed as a CDA if I work as an Aide or Assistant Teacher?**

Yes. However, you must be acting in the role of lead caregiver during the formal observation(s) by your Advisor.

C. Candidate Checklist of CDA Assessment Requirements

(Summary of activities to complete BEFORE submitting the application for CDA Assessment)

_____ Read this book carefully.

_____ Select an Advisor according to eligibility criteria.

_____ Complete the CDA Assessment Observation Instrument.

      _____ Meet with the Advisor and give her/him the *Competency Standards Book, CDA Assessment Observation Instrument for Advisors*, and the *Supplemental Observation Form*.

      _____ Discuss and schedule observation(s).

_____ Complete the Parent Opinion Questionnaires.

      _____ Distribute one questionnaire to each family.

      _____ Collect at least 75% of distributed questionnaires.

      _____ Place the sealed envelopes in a larger envelope.

      _____ Record on the outside of envelope the number of questionnaires distributed and the number collected.

_____ Complete the Professional Resource File.

      _____ Write Autobiography and make one copy to give to Council Rep.

      _____ Write Statements of Competence and make a copy to give to Council Rep.

      _____ Collect 17 Resource Items.

_____ Fill out the *Direct Assessment Application Form* and sign it.

      _____ Ask the Advisor to read and sign the Application.

      _____ Ask the Program Director to read and sign the Application; make site arrangements for the Verification Visit by the Council Rep.

_____ Attach assessment fee and training verification to Application and mail it to the Council.

Bring the following items to the Verification Visit:

      _____ The original, completed Professional Resource File

         _____ Include a copy of the *Autobiographical Statement* (to be given to the Council Rep)

         _____ Include a copy of the *Statements of Competence* (to be given to the Council Rep)

      _____ A sealed envelope containing the *CDA Assessment Observation Instrument*

      _____ A sealed envelope containing the *Parent Opinion Questionnaires*

      _____ This book

      _____ Picture identification (ID)

D. Waiver Request Form

Please fill out this form by referring to the eligibility and/or information collection requirements in the *Child Development Associate Assessment System and Competency Standards* **book.**

Candidate for CDA Assessment: _____

Last four digits of the
Social Security number: _____

Setting Type:

Center-Based Preschool ____   Center-Based Infant/Toddler ____   Family Child Care ____   Home Visitor ____

I request a waiver as [   ] Advisor or [   ] Candidate for CDA Assessment.

Eligibility or Information Collection Requirement(s) that I do not meet *(Please cite item letter and number from list of requirements):*

Qualifications I would like to substitute *(You must submit appropriate documentation supporting your waiver request):*

Please explain any special conditions:

NAME OF PERSON REQUIRING WAIVER: _____

ADDRESS: _____

_____

DAYTIME TELEPHONE: (____)_____   DATE MAILED: _____

For Council Use Only

[   ] Waiver request granted by _____   Date: _____

Waiver valid for the following period: _____ [   ] Waiver denied: _____

[   ] 12 months from the above date

[   ] One-time use, for the Candidate identified above

[   ] Other: _____

PART III
CDA Competency Standards for Preschool Caregivers in Center-Based Programs

The CDA Competency Standards are the national standards used to evaluate a caregiver's performance with children and families during the CDA assessment process. The **Competency Standards** are divided into six Competency Goals, which are statements of a general purpose or goals for caregiver behavior. The Competency Goals are common to all child care settings. The six goals are defined in more detail in 13 **Functional Areas**, which describe the major tasks or functions that a caregiver must complete in order to carry out the Competency Goal.

Each Functional Area is explained by a **developmental context**, which presents a brief overview of child development from ages 3 through 5 years and provides a rationale for the Functional Area definition and examples of competent caregiver behavior that follow.

Each Functional Area is further explained by a list of sample caregiver behaviors. These examples describe behaviors that demonstrate that a caregiver is acting in a competent way or exhibiting a skill in a particular Functional Area. During the assessment process, most Candidates will exhibit other competent behavior, and a competent Candidate might not demonstrate all the examples listed under a Functional Area. Special bilingual specialization examples are presented for several Functional Areas.

A new section "Principles for Dual Language Learners" appears at the end of the CDA Competency Standards for Preschool Caregivers in Center-Based Programs. The purpose of these principles is to provide guidance for working with preschool children whose primary (home) language is not English. A description of the developmental components of dual language acquisition emphasizes the importance of competent practices that support constructive dual language development of preschool children. Multiple examples of competent practice are presented.

The samples of caregiver competency included in the Standards should serve as a basis for recognizing other, more specific behaviors that are important to the individual Candidate. A competent Candidate might not demonstrate all the examples listed in the following pages. CDA Candidates and individuals conducting or participating in CDA training will be able to think of many different ways to demonstrate skill in the six Competency Goals and 13 Functional Areas.

Competent caregivers integrate their work and constantly adapt their skills — always thinking of the development of the whole child. In all Functional Areas, it is important for competent caregivers to individualize their work with each child while meeting the needs of the group. In every area, too, caregivers must promote multiculturalism, support families with different languages, and meet the needs of children with disabilities and special needs. And, while demonstrating skills and knowledge, competent caregivers must also demonstrate personal qualities, such as flexibility and a positive style of communicating with young children and working with families.

Competency Goal I

To establish and maintain a safe, healthy learning environment

Functional Area 1: Safe

Candidate provides a safe environment and teaches children safe practices to prevent and reduce injuries.

Developmental Context

One of the most essential services for children is to ensure their safety and well-being. Indoor and outdoor areas should be free of dangerous conditions and materials. Adults should teach children about safety and comfort children when hurt. Adults should be attentive and have the skills and knowledge to prevent injuries and to handle emergencies, accidents, and injuries appropriately when they occur.

Preschool children *(3 through 5 years old)* are gradually able to understand the relative danger or safety of situations. In a safe environment, children will gradually learn to protect themselves and look out for others.

Examples

For example, the competent Candidate working with preschool children:

- ☐ Keeps both the inside of the center and the outdoor play area free of debris, structural hazards, unguarded space heaters, tools, and dangerous substances, such as medicine, cleaning products, matches, chipping paint, toxic plants, small objects that could be swallowed, balloons, and plastic bags.

- ☐ Ensures that safety equipment, such as smoke detectors and fire extinguisher, is in place and operable and knows how to use it.

- ☐ Maintains an easily accessible and current list of phone numbers for contacting parents and emergency services, including poison control, fire company, and medical help.

☐ Uses diagrams, pictures, and words understood by children and adults to post instructions and practice procedures for fires and other emergencies, including safety procedures for children with disabilities. Involves children in setting basic safety rules. Discusses with children why a rule is needed, what might happen if children forget to follow the rule, and how the rule will keep them safe. Use visual and verbal reminders to help children remember the rule.

☐ Plans and practices monthly fire drills for moving all children in care to safety as quickly as possible.

☐ Ensures that outdoor play equipment is safe for small children and in good repair. Provides play materials related to safety. For example, includes safety road signs for block play and tricycle riding; books about walking safely in traffic.

☐ Responds immediately and sympathetically to a child's injury or fear of injury and encourages the same response by the children.

☐ Takes safety precautions in a reassuring manner without overprotecting or making children fearful.

☐ Models safety practices and gives step-by-step explanations of what and why the practices are necessary and effective.

☐ Anticipates and makes plans to prevent potentially dangerous situations, such as children being left alone or separated while on a field trip. Reviews and discusses safety rules and practices before a potentially hazardous activity or experience *(such as a cooking activity or neighborhood walk)*. Discusses the use of safe practices in context, such as when the children are using a knife to slice an apple or when stopping at the corner to watch for traffic before crossing the street.

☐ Maintains first-aid supplies *(including gauze, tape, syrup of ipecac, tweezers, scissors, and soap)* and knows basic first aid procedures appropriate for young children, such as how to handle choking, treating cuts, etc.

☐ Uses safe auto and bus travel procedures, including use of appropriate car seats for children under 4 years old and seat belts for self and other children.

☐ Discusses safety information with parents and tells them about resources, such as poison control centers, that provide services to families in their own language.

☐ Supervises all children's activities indoors and outdoors.

☐ Keeps informed about safety standards for toys and equipment and shares this information with parents.

- ☐ Helps preschoolers stop dangerous actions toward themselves and others.

- ☐ Explains cause and effect in dangerous situations in simple language, demonstrating as much as possible.

- ☐ Teaches safe use of playground equipment.

- ☐ Teaches children simple safety rules and enforces rules consistently.

- ☐ Talks and role plays with preschoolers about safety precautions.

- ☐ Adapts the indoor and outdoor environments so that children with special needs can maximize their independence (*for example, safely uses mechanical audio equipment*).

- ☐ Requires parents to authorize in writing all persons allowed to pick up children from the program.

Bilingual Specialization

In addition, the competent Candidate working towards the bilingual specialization:

- ☐ Explains and practices safety procedures such as fire drills, using the language best understood by the children.

Functional Area 2: Healthy

Candidate provides an environment that promotes health and prevents illness, and teaches children about good nutrition and practices that promote wellness.

Developmental Context

Good health involves sound medical and dental practices and good nutrition. Adults should model and encourage good health and nutrition habits with children. Food should be nutritious, prepared carefully, and served in a relaxed atmosphere. Prompt care should be given to children who are or become ill or hurt. Children need a clean environment that is properly lighted, ventilated, and heated or cooled. Indoor and outdoor areas should be free of materials or conditions that endanger children's health. Care of the child's physical needs communicates positive feelings about his/her value and influences the child's developing identity and feelings of self-worth. Parents and caregivers should exchange information about children's physical health frequently.

Children imitate and learn from the activities of those around them. Good health habits can be established through modeling and encouraging tooth brushing, hand washing, nutritious eating, etc.

Preschool children *(3 through 5 years old)* are ready to learn the reasons and take responsibility for good health practices, including good nutrition, food preparation, and tooth-brushing. They are fascinated by their own bodies and can gradually learn about them.

Examples

For example, the competent Candidate working with preschool children:

☐ Learns about good nutrition for children aged 3 through 5 years old and provides age-appropriate, nutritious meals and snacks. While respecting family customs and habits, the caregiver shares nutrition information with parents and encourages them to provide healthy foods when they contribute food to the center.

☐ Conducts activities in a positive, relaxed, and pleasant atmosphere to reduce tension and stress. Follows health and safety procedures, including proper hand washing and universal precautions.

☐ Attends to each child's physical needs, such as toileting, eating, exercising, and napping.

☐ Provides adequate ventilation and lighting, comfortable room temperatures, and good sanitation.

☐ Makes sure play areas and materials are cleaned daily.

☐ Establishes procedures for care of sick children; for example, isolating a child with a contagious illness from well children, contacting parents and medical providers, and administering medicine.

☐ Helps children develop basic health habits.

☐ Keeps handy current emergency telephone numbers for each child's parent(s), nearest relative, and medical providers.

☐ Communicates frequently with parents about children's health, nutrition, communicable diseases and medications, and cooperates with parents and health specialists.

☐ Follows center procedures for maintaining health records and administering medication and first aid and cooperates with health and nutrition staff.

☐ Establishes a relaxed mealtime routine that makes eating pleasant for each child.

☐ Limits sugar, salt, processed foods, unnecessary chemical additives, and artificial coloring and flavoring in meals and snacks and encourages parents to do the same.

☐ Informs parents about health resources, such as physicians or community clinics, that provide services to families in their primary language.

☐ Recognizes symptoms of possible abuse and neglect and is alert to play or behavior that indicates physical or sexual abuse. If physical or sexual abuse is suspected, the competent Candidate seeks out resources for information and support, follows state law in response. The Candidate responds sensitively to child's and family's needs, and cooperates in carrying out treatment plans.

☐ Uses role playing, modeling, visual material, and real objects to teach healthy physical, mental, dental, and nutritional practices.

☐ Plans health care and educational activities that integrate health and nutrition information from the children's cultures with medically accepted health and nutrition practices.

☐ Supports children in developing self-help skills in eating, toileting, washing hands, tooth-brushing, etc. Models healthy practices and gives step-by-step directions of what and why the practices are necessary and effective especially proper handwashing technique or how to sneeze into their elbows to avoid the spread of germs.

☐ Understands children's explorations, concerns, and curiosities about their own and others' bodies and responds with information at their level; for example, explaining the physical differences between boys and girls matter-of-factly in simple terms.

☐ Includes children in food preparation and provides other nutrition education activities for children.

☐ Provides opportunities for children to learn about health care by talking about visits to the doctor and dentist, reading books, and encouraging pretend play about health care.

☐ Recognizes unusual behavior and physical symptoms in children and encourages parents to obtain appropriate treatment.

☐ Works cooperatively with health professionals and parents to meet the needs of children with disabilities.

☐ Recognizes the signs of a health crisis that children with special needs may have and responds appropriately *(for example, seizures)*.

Bilingual Specialization

The competent Candidate working towards the bilingual specialization, for example:

☐ Provides written health information for parents *(for example, notices about immunizations)* in both languages.

Functional Area 3: Learning Environment

Candidate organizes and uses relationships, the physical space, materials, daily schedule, and routines to create a secure, interesting, and enjoyable environment that promotes engagement, play, exploration, and learning of all children including children with disabilities and special needs.

Developmental Context

Children of all ages learn from their own experience and by imitation. Adults can guide and encourage children's learning by ensuring that the environment is emotionally supportive; invites active exploration, play, and movement by children; and supports a broad array of experiences. A reliable routine together with a stimulating choice of materials, activities, and relationships enhances children's learning and development.

Preschool children *(3 through 5 years old)* are developing new language skills, physical control, and awareness of themselves and others each day. They enjoy participation in planned and group activities, but they are not yet ready to sit still or work in a group for very long. They learn by doing. Adults can support their learning in all areas by maintaining an environment that is dependable but flexible enough to provide opportunities for them to extend their skills, understanding, and judgment in individualized ways. Adults can observe children's play; give them time and space to repeat familiar activities; and expand the learning environment in response to their developing skills, interest, and concerns about themselves and their world.

Examples

For example, the competent Candidate working with preschool children:

☐ Uses materials, books, and equipment that are interesting and developmentally appropriate for each child, including those of children with special needs.

☐ Uses materials that demonstrate acceptance of each child's sex, family, race, language, religion, and culture.

☐ Arranges the environment to help children do their best. For example, makes sure block building has enough space and is protected from traffic; avoids arrangements that invite children to run or fight such as long corridors or large open spaces.

☐ Locates quiet areas, such as the book, art, or writing centers next to each other, separated from noisier and more active centers such as blocks, dramatic play, or woodworking.

☐ Organizes the physical space into learning centers that allow children to independently choose their own activities for part of each day. If children have difficulty, at first limits their choices and then gradually adds more offerings.

☐ Establishes clear boundaries between learning centers by using furniture, floor coverings, or shelves that help limit the number of children who work or play in each area at one time.

☐ Locates messy activities such as sand and water play, and art near a source of water for easy access and cleanup.

☐ Provides sufficient space, toys and equipment for child-initiated physical activities outdoors.

☐ Offers sufficient indoor space for activities so children can move without getting in each other's way.

☐ Plans schedule for a balance of learning experiences: large group, small group, and individualized; child-initiated and teacher-initiated; active and quiet; indoor and outdoor.

☐ Provides a comfortable meeting space for the whole group to engage in music, movement, book reading and other large group activities; designate seating arrangements so children are not crowded or distracted by toys within reach.

☐ Plans for 60 to 75 minutes for center/choice time so children can become deeply engaged in teacher-supported play and projects. *(In a full-day program, allow at least 60 minutes in the morning and another in the afternoon.)*

☐ Limits whole group meeting times to 10 to 20 minutes and give opportunities for children to be actively engaged during these experiences.

☐ Prepares ahead of time for the next activity so children do not spend excessive amounts of time waiting.

☐ Minimizes the number of transitions between activities and the amount of time children spend in transitions. Gives children a warning before a transition happens, such as "Five more minutes till cleanup time." For those children who have particular difficulty with transitions, gives them an individual warning and explanation of what is to come.

☐ Makes transitions learning experiences by singing songs, reciting rhymes or poems, counting steps, following the leader's motions, doing movement exercises, or following specific directions such as, "If your name starts with a K, get your coat."

☐ Uses routines such as snack and mealtimes, cleanup, brushing teeth, washing hands, dressing for outdoors, or rest time as learning opportunities (sitting and talking with children during meals and snacks) and for children to practice newly acquired skills.

☐ Provides many opportunities for children to develop their senses and ability to concentrate.

☐ Varies routines spontaneously to take advantage of unusual opportunities; for example, goes outside in the snow, invites a visiting grandmother to share stories or songs with children, lets the children watch workers and machinery on the street, or plays with one child for an extra period of time when additional adults are available to care for group.

☐ Adapts the daily schedule to accommodate individual children's needs and interests, including children with disabilities and special needs, rather than requiring them to fit the schedule.

Bilingual Specialization

In addition, the competent Candidate working towards the bilingual specialization, for example:

☐ Uses objects, music activities, and celebrations that are meaningful to young children to encourage development of both languages and cultures.

☐ Helps parents identify resources in their homes, families, and community that will support the development of both languages.

☐ Establishes and maintains a routine for use of the second language in daily activities.

Competency Goal II

To advance physical and intellectual competence

Functional Area 4:   Physical

Candidate uses a variety of developmentally appropriate equipment, learning experiences, and teaching strategies to promote the physical development (fine motor and gross motor) of all children.

Developmental Context

Physical development is an essential part of the total development of children. Developing physically includes using large and small muscles, coordinating movements, and using the senses. Large-motor development includes strengthening and coordinating the muscles and nervous system, controlling large motions using the arms, legs, torso, or whole body. Small-motor development involves the ability to control and coordinate small, specialized motions using the eyes, mouth, hands, and feet. Adults should provide materials, equipment, and opportunities for indoor and outdoor activities that encourage this development and recognize and respect the wide differences in individual rates of physical development.

Preschool children *(3 through 5 years old)* are gradually refining new skills: skipping, drawing, threading, throwing, and catching. They are interested in learning subtle differences through their senses: sweet and sour, rough and smooth, high and low, loud and soft. They can attend and persist for longer periods of time when they are absorbed in using their small muscles on a puzzle or an art project. They also need daily opportunities to exercise their large muscles in free play and organized activities. Daily physical activities can promote children's cognitive, creative, and language growth, as well as their physical development.

Examples

For example, the competent Candidate working with preschool children:

- ☐ Arranges and encourages physical activities, knowing how children's physical development affects their cognitive, social, and emotional development.

☐ Observes and evaluates children's developmental levels in order to provide activities for physical skills and development of the senses that are achievable and also challenging for each child.

☐ Provides materials for a range of fine motor skill levels. For example, includes table blocks in several sizes, puzzles with different numbers of pieces *(e.g., 15 to 50 pieces, depending on children's abilities)*, software with several levels of complexity.

☐ Offers and adapts learning experiences to allow children with different levels of fine motor skills and children with disabilities to participate with success. For example, while making a group collage, children can tear or cut pieces of paper to add to the creation.

☐ Plans group and individual routines that allow children to be actively involved. Makes sure the schedule provides enough time for children's participation. For example, children can fold napkins; put on and take off coats, hats, and boots; mix paint and wash paintbrushes; and pour from small pitchers.

☐ Observes children using fine motor skills and use appropriate teaching behaviors as needed such as modeling how to hold a hammer, or giving instruction on how to use an eggbeater.

☐ Keeps track of each child's fine motor abilities and offer materials, equipment, and opportunities that allow the child to practice on their own. Offers challenges that will help the child progress without getting frustrated.

☐ Follows a daily schedule that allows children to spend ample time each day in structured and unstructured physical activity, allowing children to alternate using their gross motor skills in physical activities with opportunities to rest and recover energy.

☐ Plans structured physical activities that introduce a variety of movement skills individually, with a partner, and in a small group. For example, may offer balls of different sizes and materials *(e.g., rubber, foam, inflatable plastic)*, to roll, kick, throw, or catch; plan balancing activities.

☐ Participates in physical activities with children, modeling movement skills, offering individualized assistance, learning how children approach and respond to physical challenges, and encouraging children to practice and refine their skills *(for example, playing ball, running, jumping, climbing with children, both indoors and outdoors)*.

☐ Provides a variety of activities from children's culture(s), such as dances, music, fingerplays, and active games.

☐ Provides opportunities for children to develop their senses by noticing colors, smelling odors, distinguishing sounds, feeling and touching a variety of objects, and tasting different foods.

☐ Communicates to children and their parents the importance of outdoor play and physical activity for healthy growth and development.

☐ Supports and encourages, but does not force, children who are fearful of physical activity because of illness, accidents, abuse, limited opportunity, or overprotective caregivers and parents.

☐ Observes and evaluates children's physical development, recognizes signs of possible physical disabilities and developmental delays, refers parents to appropriate services, and follows up on referrals or individual development plans.

☐ Adapts the program to meet the special needs of children with disabilities, taking into account the importance of physical development to self-concept and social development.

☐ Avoids overprotecting children with disabilities, supports their independent functioning, includes them in physical activities with other children *(making modifications only when necessary)*, and encourages parents to do the same.

> ## Functional Area 5: Cognitive
>
> *Candidate uses a variety of developmentally appropriate learning experiences and teaching strategies to promote curiosity, reasoning, and problem-solving, and to lay the foundation for all later learning. Candidate implements curriculum that promotes children's learning of important mathematics, science, technology, social studies, and other content goals.*

Developmental Context

Exploring and trying to understand the world is natural and necessary for children's cognitive or intellectual development. As children learn and grow, their thinking capacities expand and become more flexible. Adults should support and guide this process by building on children's interests with new learning opportunities and to their questions, with information and enthusiasm. Cognitive development also requires healthy development in other areas: consistent physical growth, secure emotional behavior, and positive social interaction.

Preschool children *(3 through 5 years old)* continue their cognitive development through actively exploring their world and manipulating objects, thinking and solving problems, talking and engaging with adults and other children in a variety of roles, and repeating and practicing their learning. Their increasing ability to describe objects and experiences with words reinforces their understanding of abstract concepts. Adults can expand learning through play, introduce a variety of new opportunities for learning, and ensure that preschoolers experience a balance of challenge and success.

Examples

For example, the competent Candidate working with preschool children:

☐ Observes children's play and interactions frequently to assess their cognitive development and readiness for new challenges and learning opportunities.

☐ Uses a variety of learning experiences and teaching strategies that engage children's curiosity, inventiveness, and problem-solving and communication skills.

☐ Provides opportunities for children to try out and begin to understand the relationships between cause and effect and means and ends.

☐ Understands the importance of play and often joins children's play as a partner and facilitator.

☐ Uses the center environment, everyday activities, and homemade materials to encourage children's intellectual development.

☐ Uses traditional and emerging technologies *(e.g., computers, digital media and cameras, Internet, microscopes, and videotapes)* in a developmentally appropriate way to support and extend learning across the curriculum.

☐ Provides opportunities for children to engage with high quality digital media resources individually, with peers, and with caregivers or parents.

☐ Ensures that all children (i.e., both genders and children with disabilities and special needs) have equal access to high quality technology resources.

☐ Helps children discover ways to solve problems that arise in daily activities.

☐ Supports children's repetitions of the familiar and introduces new experiences, activities, and materials when children are interested and ready.

☐ Recognizes individual differences and finds ways to work effectively with each child.

☐ Encourages active learning, rather than emphasizing that children listen passively to adults.

☐ Provides equipment and materials that children can explore and master by themselves.

☐ Is alert to the task a child is attempting and provides appropriate support.

☐ Models curiosity, inquiry, and investigation for children. Encourages children to ask questions and seek help and responds to them in ways that extend their thinking; for example, "That's a good question; let's see if we can find out."

☐ Asks questions that have more than one answer, encouraging children to wonder, guess, and talk about their ideas; for example, "What do you think might happen if … ?" or "How do you feel when … ?"

☐ Listens to children and encourages them to talk about their experiences and observations.

☐ Provides opportunities to organize and group, compare and contrast thoughts, words, objects, and sensations.

☐ Involves children in projects such as cooking, gardening, and repairing, when possible.

☐ Reduces distractions and interruptions so that children have opportunities to extend their attention span and work on one activity, such as block building or water play, for a long period of time.

☐ Incorporates mathematics and science concepts and skills during projects and as children play with blocks, water, sand, playdough and other materials; dramatic play, cooking, art, music and movement, stories, and outdoor experiences.

☐ Uses planned and everyday experiences to promote mathematics concepts by posing questions such as "Do we have enough chairs for everyone?"

☐ Builds on and extends children's knowledge and understanding of their world by using information books, field trips (including virtual field trips), visitors, and other ways of opening up the classroom.

☐ Helps children learn mathematics and science vocabulary by introducing it into their play and other activities, regularly using words such as *more than, less than, about, near, approximately,* and *in between.*

☐ Obtains (or makes) and uses special learning materials and equipment to maximize participation and learning of children with disabilities and special needs.

☐ Recognizes potential learning problems and collects good observational examples to support concerns.

☐ Uses written observational examples of children to make and support referrals according to center policy.

Bilingual Specialization

In addition, the competent Candidate working towards the bilingual specialization, for example:

☐ Provides learning experiences that lead to the understanding of basic concepts in the language most familiar to each child.

☐ Encourages learning of both languages through everyday experiences and activities.

Functional Area 6: Communication

Candidate uses a variety of developmentally appropriate learning experiences and teaching strategies to promote children's language and early literacy learning, and help them communicate their thoughts and feelings verbally and nonverbally. Candidate helps dual-language learners make progress in understanding and speaking both English and their home language.

Developmental Context

Communication between people can take many forms, including spoken and written words or sounds, gestures, eye and body movements, and touch. Children need to understand verbal and nonverbal means of communicating thoughts, feelings, and ideas. Adults can help children develop their communication skills by encouraging communication and providing ample opportunity for children to listen, interact, and express themselves freely with other children and adults.

Preschool children *(3 through 5 years old)* develop a wide range of abilities to communicate both verbally and nonverbally. Adults should communicate actively with each child — modeling good speech, listening carefully, responding actively to their expressions, engaging in conversations with them, and building on their verbal and nonverbal understanding and vocabulary. During the preschool years, early literacy experiences provide the foundation for later success in learning to read and write.

Examples

For example, the competent Candidate working with preschool children:

- ☐ Has realistic expectations for each child's understanding and use of speech based on knowledge of language development and the individual child.

- ☐ Engages in one-to-one, extended conversations with individual children about their personal experiences or events in the program.

- ☐ Listens to children with respect, giving them time — five seconds or so — to respond to a question or conversational comment.

- ☐ Responds to children's speech with expansions and questions, and introduces and explains new words to expand vocabulary.

☐ Provides a good language model for children, using standard grammatical speech. Recognizes that many of children's errors (*I wented to the store,* or *three sheeps*) show their efforts to learn a rule, like the *s* of the possessive, which they overgeneralize. Instead of correcting the child, picks up on what he says but says it correctly. *(For example, a child may say, "I gots two foots" and the teacher replies, "Yes, you have two feet so you need two socks.")*

☐ Talks with children about events, experiences, or people that are beyond the here and now — events from the past, the future, or children's imaginations.

☐ Participates in play to get it going if children have difficulty, or to extend it to give children opportunities to practice verbal interaction with other children and occasionally with adults. For instance, enters the play restaurant and pretends to be a customer, "Could I see a menu, please? I'd like to order dinner."

☐ Provides activities that encourage children to develop listening and comprehension skills.

☐ Helps children connect word meaning(s) to experiences and real objects.

☐ Recognizes, understands, and respects local speech patterns and idioms.

☐ Respects the language of non-English-speaking families, encourages them to communicate freely with their children in the language parents prefer, and helps them find opportunities to learn English.

☐ Is aware of the caregiver's role as a language model for children and uses affectionate and playful tones, clear speech, and responsive conversation.

☐ Listens attentively to children, tries to understand what they want to communicate, and helps them to express themselves. Encourages children to take turns talking and listening instead of interrupting each other or adults and ensures that each child has a chance to talk.

☐ Recognizes possible impairments or delays that affect hearing and speech, works with appropriate professionals and families to find resources, implement treatment plans, and communicate effectively with these children.

☐ Shares children's communication/language achievements with parents.

☐ Uses a variety of songs, stories, books, and games — including those from the children's cultures — for language development and learning early literacy skills such as phonological awareness.

☐ Reads to children every day with the express purpose of enhancing their vocabulary and listening skills. Regularly reads in small groups of 4 to 6 to ensure children's active participation.

☐ Actively engages children in book reading time — asking questions about the book before reading it *(such as where is the cover or title)* or posing questions that call on them to predict what will happen or notice cause-effect relationships; and chanting with rhyme and patterns.

☐ Creates a comfortable library area, displaying books attractively on open shelves, with covers facing front, accessible for children to make their selections.

☐ Makes sure that books in the classroom reflect children's culture, home language, and identity.

☐ Plans times during the day when children select their own books to look at alone or with a friend.

☐ Writes down children's messages to parents or others, dictations for language experience charts, or stories, and read them back.

☐ Provides a print-rich environment *(meaningful signs, labels)* including a well-stocked writing center.

☐ Engages children in their own writing of signs or labels using pictures, letter-like symbols, letters and their own "kid-writing". Displays at eye level the alphabet and functional print such as children's names, classroom jobs for the week, or daily schedule. Displays letters where children see, touch and manipulate them *(for example, magnetic or sandpaper letters)*, and use them where they work and play.

☐ Helps children take the next step beyond what they are currently capable of doing *(that is, provide scaffolding)*. For example, if a child has been writing his name with just a J for several weeks, asks, "What comes after your J, Jamal?" and shows him the next letter if he doesn't know it.

☐ Provides opportunities for children to represent their ideas nonverbally through activities such as painting, making music, and creative movement.

Bilingual Specialization

In addition, the competent Candidate working towards a bilingual specialization, for example:

☐ Demonstrates ability to understand, speak, read, and write both languages.

☐ Understands the principles and characteristics of bilingual language development in children and explains these to parents.

☐ Assesses each child's language abilities and uses activities that are appropriate to the child's level of development in each language.

☐ Helps children associate word meanings in both languages with familiar objects and experiences.

☐ Encourages children who are fluent in either language to help less fluent children.

☐ Helps parents understand the importance of children's learning the first language and culture and their role in providing experiences to meet this goal.

☐ Helps parents understand the child's attempts at communication in the second language.

☐ Allows children opportunities to express themselves in the language of their choice.

☐ Encourages English-speaking children and families to learn the second language.

☐ Uses lullabies, songs, games, stories, books, and fingerplays, from both languages, asking parents for examples from their childhood.

☐ Makes sure there are consistent language models for both languages used in the program, through selection and use of materials and personnel.

Functional Area 7: Creative

Candidate uses a variety of developmentally appropriate learning experiences and teaching strategies for children to explore music, movement, and the visual arts, and to develop and express their individual creative abilities.

Developmental Context

All children are imaginative and have creative potential. They need opportunities to develop and express these capacities. Creative play serves many purposes for children in their cognitive, social, physical, and emotional development. Adults should support the development of children's creative impulses by respecting creative play and by providing a wide variety of activities and materials that encourage spontaneous expression and expand children's imagination.

Preschool children *(3 through 5 years old)* can express their creativity in increasingly symbolic ways through the use of their bodies, words, and materials (building blocks, music, dance, art) and through make-believe. Adults can promote creativity by providing space, time, and materials for children to create and recreate their individual works, their own dramas, and their unique solutions to problems and by respecting the process of creativity as much as the product.

Examples

For example, the competent Candidate working with preschool children:

- ☐ Recognizes that the process of creating is as important — and sometimes more important — than the product.

- ☐ Understands that each child's creative expression is unique and does not encourage uniformity.

- ☐ Allows time for spontaneous and extended play within the daily routine.

- ☐ Includes a variety of music, art, literature, dance, role playing, celebrations, and other creative activities from the children's culture(s) in program activities.

- ☐ Participates in make-believe games with children.

- ☐ Models and encourages children's creativity in language; for example, through rhymes, imaginative stories, and nonsense words.

☐ Provides unstructured materials (such as blocks, paint, clay, or musical instruments).

☐ Encourages thorough, repeated exploration of creative materials whenever possible; for example, by letting a block structure stand so that building can continue the next day or by letting one child play with soap suds for an extended period of time.

☐ Models creativity by using homemade materials and found objects.

☐ Helps parents understand the importance of creative expression in children's development and the need to provide children with opportunities for creative activities such as storytelling, playing make-believe, using art materials.

☐ Provides for "messy" activities with children, such as water and sand play, finger painting, and drawing with markers.

☐ Encourages children to try new and different activities.

☐ Provides and rotates a variety of male and female dress-up clothes and other "props," including those from the children's culture(s).

☐ Keeps informed about cultural resources in the community and uses them with children when possible.

☐ Provides crayons, paper, paste, and scissors in a place where children can use them independently.

☐ Models open-mindedness and creativity. Demonstrates that there may be more than one way to do things or to solve problems.

☐ Provides a wide variety of open-ended materials and tools children can explore and use to create art and other work.

☐ When introducing a new material and technique, demonstrates how use it, such as how to work with real potter's clay.

☐ Teaches children how to use materials that might be challenging, such as how to hammer a nail.

☐ Encourages children by making positive, specific comments rather than empty praise. Instead of, "What a pretty painting", says "I see you mixed blue and yellow together." Asks open-ended questions, such as "How did you make this pattern?"

☐ Uses various art forms, materials, and techniques representing children's cultures.

☐ Treats children's work with respect, displaying at eye-level, in a variety of places throughout the classroom and sending art home to share with families.

☐ Offers sufficient space for creating and storing completed work and work-in-progress.

☐ Engages children in making and listening to music, incorporating the music of children's cultures and home languages in the curriculum.

☐ Shares and discusses a variety of musical forms and styles.

Bilingual Specialization

In addition, the competent Candidate working towards the bilingual specialization, for example:

☐ Helps children develop creative abilities through activities and discussion in both languages.

☐ Helps children identify and imitate creative forms found in the art, music, and dance of their cultures.

Competency Goal III

To support social and emotional development and to provide positive guidance

Functional Area 8: Self

Candidate develops a warm, positive, supportive, and responsive relationship with each child, and helps each child learn about and take pride in his or her individual and cultural identity.

Developmental Context

All children need a physically and emotionally secure environment that supports their developing self-knowledge, self-regulation, and self-esteem and, at the same time, encourages respect for the feelings and rights of others. Knowing oneself includes knowing about one's body, feelings, and abilities. It also means identifying oneself as a girl or boy and a member of a family and a larger cultural community. Accepting and taking pride in oneself comes from experiencing success and being accepted by others as a unique individual. Self-esteem develops as children master new abilities, experience success as well as failure, and realize their effectiveness in handling increasingly challenging demands in their own ways.

Like toddlers, healthy **preschool children** *(3 through 5 years old)* experience many conflicting feelings and ideas: independence and dependence, confidence and doubt, fear and power, hostility and love, anger and tenderness, and aggression and passivity. They continue to need a reliable environment and secure relationships with adults as they deal with these feelings and learn more about themselves in an expanding world: peers, school, neighborhood, and society. They are proud of their new skill in caring for themselves, developing friendships, building and making things work, understanding, and achieving. Adults can support them by respecting and recognizing the strengths and needs of each child and by providing experiences that help them grow as individuals.

Examples

For example, the competent Candidate working with preschool children:

☐ Gets to know each child, establishes relationships with families, and finds out about unique strengths, needs, interests, and abilities. Treats each child as an individual.

☐ Establishes positive, warm, caring relationships with each child, including those children with disabilities and special needs.

☐ Greets children personally each day when they arrive, addresses each child by name, talks with each child every day at their eye level, and encourages each child to call other children and adults by name.

☐ Shows respect and warmth to all children through physical affection, a soothing tone of voice, smiles and laughter, acknowledges accomplishments with nods, smiles, hugs, high-fives, or thumbs-up.

☐ Prominently displays photos of children and family members, children's work, and children's names.

☐ Encourages children to do for themselves what they are capable of doing whether it is dressing, serving snack, cleaning up, writing their names, solving a problem, and other ways of demonstrating growing competence.

☐ Makes sure the learning environment is welcoming to every child and reflects his or her identity and culture.

☐ Is sensitive to differing cultural values and expectations concerning behavior, independence, and expression of feelings.

☐ Helps children through periods of stress, separation, transition, and other crises.

☐ When possible, offers children choices in activities, materials, and foods and respects their choices.

☐ Gives one-to-one attention to each child as much as possible.

☐ Enjoys children and directly expresses the enjoyment to them.

☐ Delights in each child's success, expresses kindness and support when a child is having trouble, and helps him/her learn from mistakes.

☐ Helps children recognize and accept their feelings, such as joy, affection, anger, jealousy, sadness, and fear, and express feelings in culturally appropriate ways.

☐ Models the recognition and expression of feelings by naming her/his own feelings while expressing them.

☐ Supports child's developing awareness of him/herself as a member of a family and of an ethnic or social group by talking about families *(using photographs, mirrors, or other appropriate objects)* and by celebrating cultural events with children.

☐ Uses books, pictures, stories, and discussion to help children identify positively with the events and experiences of their lives; for example, single-parent families, extended families, divorce, moving, or birth of siblings.

☐ Comments directly, sincerely, and positively to children about their performance and ideas.

☐ Helps children recognize and appreciate racial, ethnic, and ability differences and similarities.

☐ Emphasizes cooperation in games and activities so that each child experiences success.

☐ Talks with children about "good touching" and "bad touching" as a way of preventing sexual abuse.

☐ Provides many opportunities for all children, including those with disabling conditions, to feel effective, experience success, and gain the positive recognition of others.

☐ Understands the effect of abuse and neglect on children's self-concept and works sensitively with such children.

Bilingual Specialization

In addition, the competent Candidate working towards a bilingual specialization, for example:

☐ Helps children feel good about themselves as speakers of each language.

☐ Supports the child's attempt to use the second language.

☐ Helps each child deal with the stress of separation, using the child's first language and a tone and style compatible with the family's.

Functional Area 9:   Social

Candidate helps each child function effectively in the group, learn to express feelings, acquire social skills, and make friends, and promotes mutual respect among children and adults.

Developmental Context

Children need to develop social skills that help them make friends, work and play cooperatively and productively with other children and adults. To do this, children need to feel secure about themselves, value other people, and enjoy positive social interaction.

Preschool children *(3 through 5 years old)* welcome social interactions with adults and children. Their social skills develop rapidly, first in periods of parallel play and gradually through more cooperative play. Adults can promote understanding and respect among preschool children by providing experiences in sharing materials, responsibilities, and social problem solving. Preschoolers can begin to learn about differing individual and group needs in a positive way.

Examples

For example, the competent Candidate working with preschool children:

- ☐ Learns about children's social development and helps children and parents deal with such typical issues as separation anxiety, negative behavior, shyness, sexual identity, and making friends.

- ☐ Has realistic expectations for young children's social behavior based on their level of development.

- ☐ Serves as a social model by building a positive relationship with each child and parent and by maintaining positive relationships with other adults in the center.

- ☐ Responds quickly and calmly to prevent children from hurting each other.

- ☐ Helps children learn to respect the rights and possessions of others, in light of local expectations regarding sharing.

- ☐ Encourages children to ask for, accept, and give help to one another.

- ☐ Encourages and supports children to make friends, especially those who are isolated from or rejected by peers.

☐ Helps the children become aware of their feelings and those of others by talking about feelings with each child.

☐ Encourages play and relationships among all children across racial, language, ethnic, age, and gender groupings, including children with disabilities and special needs.

☐ Encourages children to express their feelings and assert rights in socially acceptable ways.

☐ Encourages children to comfort and help one another.

☐ Teaches children conflict resolution skills and encourages them to practice these skills.

☐ Encourages cooperation rather than competition.

☐ Helps children recognize their own and others' feelings, similarities, and differences and helps them empathize with others.

☐ Helps all children feel valued as members of the group.

☐ Encourages children to share stories and activities from their families and cultures.

☐ Uses stories, pictures, and other materials to teach children social skills and about issues such as sharing, separation, negative behavior, and disabilities.

Bilingual Specialization

In addition, the competent Candidate working towards a bilingual specialization, for example:

☐ Understands that the social roles and expectations for bilingual children in their family setting may be different from those of the child care program and helps the children to behave appropriately in each.

Functional Area 10: Guidance

Candidate provides a supportive environment and uses effective strategies to promote children's self-regulation and support acceptable behaviors, and effectively intervenes for children with persistent challenging behaviors.

Developmental Context

Knowing what behavior is appropriate or acceptable in a situation is an important skill. Children develop this understanding when consistent limits and realistic expectations of their behavior are clearly and positively defined. Understanding and following simple rules can help children develop self-regulation, the ability to regulate their behavior and emotions according to the demands of the situation. Children feel more secure when they know what is expected of them and when adult expectations realistically take into account each child's development and needs.

Preschool children *(3 through 5 years old)* can participate in the process of setting group rules and can benefit from learning why they are necessary. They require an understanding caregiver who remains calm and supportive during their continuing struggle to become self-regulated. They will continue to "test" limits from time to time as they grow more confident and independent. Adults can support them by acknowledging their feelings and remaining consistent about expectations, routines, and limits.

Examples

For example, the competent Candidate working with preschool children:

- ☐ Knows a variety of positive guidance methods — such as listening, reinforcement, and redirection — and uses each appropriately.

- ☐ Teaches children positive alternatives to socially unacceptable behavior.

- ☐ Relates guidance practices to knowledge of each child's personality and level of development.

- ☐ Does not use negative methods, such as spanking, threatening, shouting, isolating, or shaming children.

- ☐ Establishes guidelines for children's behavior that encourage self-regulation and that are clear, reasonable, and consistent.

☐ Alerts children to changes in activities or routines well in advance and handles transitions from one activity to another with clear directions and patience.

☐ Is able to modify play when it becomes overstimulating for any of the children, including children with disabilities.

☐ Builds a trusting relationship with children as a foundation for positive guidance and self-discipline.

☐ Anticipates confrontations between children and defuses provocative behavior.

☐ Addresses the problem behavior or situation rather than labeling the child involved.

☐ Helps parents develop realistic expectations for children's behavior in ways that help avoid disciplinary problems *(for example, discussing how long children usually can sit still, attend, or persist).*

☐ Encourages parents to talk about childrearing, guidance, and self-discipline and refers them to classes, books, and other resources, as appropriate.

☐ Knows parents' disciplinary methods and expectations and selects those appropriate for use in the center.

☐ Has realistic expectations about children's attention spans, interests, social abilities, and physical needs, including children with disabilities.

☐ Gives children real choices and accepts the choices made: for example, "Do you want to read a book with me or play on the climber?" or "Shall we have the apples or bananas for snack today?"

☐ Lets children solve their own problems whenever possible.

☐ Explains the reasons for rules in clear language, demonstrating whenever possible.

☐ Uses firm and friendly techniques, such as reminding and persuading, when rules are forgotten or disobeyed.

☐ Uses positive language with children: for example, "walk" rather than "don't run."

☐ Involves children in establishing guidelines and limits.

☐ Recognizes that sometimes serious behavior problems are related to developmental or emotional problems and works cooperatively with parents and other professionals towards solutions.

☐ Works with families and a team of specialists to implement a positive behavior plan and systematic intervention strategies for children with persistent challenging behavior.

☐ Is aware of each child's limitations and abilities, uses guidance techniques accordingly, and explains rules at the child's level of understanding

Bilingual Specialization

In addition, the competent Candidate working towards a bilingual specialization, for example:

☐ Uses the language in which each child understands expectations, limits, and guidance.

Competency Goal IV

To establish positive and productive relationships with families

Functional Area 11: Families

Candidate establishes a positive, responsive, cooperative relationship with each child's family, engages in two-way communication with families, encourages their involvement in the program, and supports the child's relationship with his or her family.

Developmental Context

Today's families take many different forms. Each family has primary responsibility for its own children, and parents may share this responsibility for their children with others. The parents and the caregiver become partners who communicate respectfully and openly for the mutual benefit of the children, the family, and the caregiver. Caregivers also recognize that parenthood, too, is a developmental process and that they can support parents in their role.

Preschool children *(3 through 5 years old)* move back and forth from family to the child care program more independently than younger children. They are also more sensitive to the differences between the two environments and observe interactions between their parents and caregivers carefully. Parents and caregivers should keep each other informed of important developments in the children's lives and provide mutual support in nurturing their physical, social, emotional, and intellectual development.

Examples

☐ For example, the competent Candidate working with preschool children:

☐ Recognizes that children's primary caregivers may be single mothers or fathers, two parents of the same or opposite sex, stepparents, grandparents, uncles, aunts, sisters, brothers, foster parents, or guardians.

☐ Helps parents understand the development of their child and understand the child's point of view.

☐ Regularly shares information with families via two-way communication (parents and teachers listen to and learn from each other). Includes parents in establishing goals for the program and for their children's learning and development.

☐ Welcomes parents as visitors at all times.

☐ Finds meaningful ways to involve families in the program. Encourages parents to visit the center, participate in activities, and make suggestions for the daily program.

☐ Regularly holds parent conferences during which both parties share information about children's progress at home and in the program.

☐ Conducts home visits or if parents prefer, meets privately with them at a comfortable site such as a library or local community center.

☐ Negotiates openly any areas of discomfort or parental concern. Respects and tries to understand the parents' views when they differ from the program's goals or policies and attempts to resolve the differences.

☐ Demonstrates respect for various cultures and languages, making sure that children's home languages and cultures are reflected in books, signs, and learning experiences.

☐ Respects parents' authority and preferences for their child, and each family's cultural background, religious belief, and childrearing practices.

☐ Offers parents information about health and social services and other resources in the community.

☐ Observes strict confidentiality regarding children and families, except as required by laws for reporting child abuse and neglect, and makes parents aware of this policy.

☐ Suggests activities and materials that parents can share with their children at home.

☐ Encourages parents to talk about important family events and their children's special interests and behavior at home. Shares information frequently with parents about the child's experiences in the center.

☐ Is able to discuss learning challenges or problem behavior with parents in a constructive, supportive manner.

☐ Supports parents in making arrangements for school or an alternative child care program, when necessary. Works with parents to prepare children for entering school or making transitions.

☐ Develops attachment towards children without competing with parents.

☐ Tells parents about children's achievements and shares their pleasure in new abilities.

☐ Helps parents with separations from child, recognizing parents' possible concerns about leaving their child.

☐ Supports children and families under stress, working cooperatively with other professionals, as appropriate.

☐ Sends home projects made by the children.

☐ Helps parents find ways to enjoy time with their preschoolers and to help them relax after time in a group setting.

☐ Supports child's sense of belonging to his/her family.

☐ Helps parents understand the importance of play for preschool children.

☐ Shares information with parents about the learning opportunities for children in everyday household tasks and routines.

☐ Helps parents recognize their feelings and attitudes about disabilities.

☐ Works with other staff members and families as part of a team to help identify, diagnose, and implement individualized plans for children with disabilities and special needs.

☐ Shares with parents clear and understandable information about their children's disabilities and information about the family's legal right to services.

☐ Encourages and assists parents to communicate confidently about their children with government and other community agencies.

Bilingual Specialization

In addition, the competent Candidate working towards a bilingual specialization, for example:

☐ Regularly communicates orally and in writing with parents and children in their preferred language.

□ Helps parents understand the program goals for bilingual development.

□ Knows parents' views on such issues as the use of first and second languages within the program, childrearing, and biculturalism and incorporates their views into program planning.

□ Regularly communicates with parents about their child's bilingual development and helps them find ways to support this within the family.

□ Supports families' desire to communicate their language and cultural heritage to their children through cultural practices.

Competency Goal V

*To ensure a well-run, purposeful program responsive
to participant needs*

Functional Area 12: Program Management

Candidate is a manager who uses observation, documentation, and planning to support children's development and learning and to ensure effective operation of the classroom or group. The Candidate is a competent organizer, planner, recordkeeper, communicator, and a cooperative co-worker.

Developmental Context

Running an effective program requires a systematic approach. A systematic approach means that the Candidate can determine the needs of her/his operation, families, and children; can make plans based on those needs; and can keep accurate records of needs, plans, and practices. Such a systematic approach should be applied to keeping records of attendance, fees, health status, and home visits. It should include specific plans for meeting the needs of children and their families and coordinating communication among involved adults through written information, meetings with parents and resource persons, and frequent informal discussions.

Examples

For example, the competent Candidate working with preschool children:

☐ Uses multiple means of assessing, observing, and documenting children's development and learning including information from parents to identify the strengths, interests, abilities, and needs of each child.

☐ Develops skills in observing and recording information about children and their families in a nonjudgmental manner for use in planning and carrying out daily programs.

☐ Maintains up-to-date records concerning the growth, health, behavior, and progress of each child and the group and shares the information with parents and appropriate center personnel.

☐ Considers goals and objectives for each child and for the group as a whole. Develops realistic plans responsive to the needs of all, including children with disabilities.

☐ Prepares and implements plans for individual children and the group by identifying developmentally and culturally appropriate learning experiences and materials for each day.

☐ Has a clear understanding of her/his responsibilities within the program.

☐ Discusses issues that affect the program with appropriate staff and follows up on their resolution.

☐ Works as a member of a team with others in the classroom and the program, including substitutes, parents and volunteers.

☐ Supports other staff by offering assistance and supervision when needed.

☐ Makes or obtains materials and equipment appropriate to the developmental needs of the children.

☐ Coordinates program plans *(including guidance and discipline techniques)* with parents, specialists, and program personnel, when appropriate.

☐ Knows the language resources of each family and uses these in the program.

☐ Works with appropriate staff to choose substitutes carefully, requiring experience with children of the same ages whenever possible.

☐ Orients new or substitute caregivers and volunteers to routines and the special needs and abilities of each child.

☐ Implements procedures that help children make a smooth transition from one group to another.

☐ Knows the social service, health, and education resources of the community and uses them when appropriate.

☐ Recognizes possible learning problems and works with parents and specialists to develop plans specific to the needs of each child. Implements recommended treatment by the following up on referrals, and working with the family to meet goals for the child.

☐ Establishes liaison with community services that respond to family violence *(for example, Parents Anonymous, Child Protective Services, and local shelter programs).*

Bilingual Specialization

In addition, the competent Candidate working towards a bilingual specialization, for example:

☐ Uses knowledge of language development and bilingualism to plan for each child and the group.

☐ Recognizes and helps others recognize the needs of children and families who speak a different language and operate in a different cultural context.

☐ Makes use of available evaluation instruments in the non-English language.

☐ Takes account of families' concerns about such issues as language usage and culturally different styles of relating.

☐ Works with appropriate staff in choosing substitutes who meet the language needs of the children and program whenever possible.

Competency Goal VI
To maintain a commitment to professionalism

Functional Area 13: Professionalism

Candidate makes decisions based on knowledge of research-based early childhood practices, promotes high-quality in child care services, and takes advantage of opportunities to improve knowledge and competence, both for personal and professional growth and for the benefit of children and families.

Developmental Context

Professionals working with young children and their families make decisions based on knowledge of early childhood education and family life and demonstrate a commitment towards high quality care for young children. The professional caregiver continues to set new goals and take advantage of educational experiences that will help her/him to grow more competent. Recognizing that the way they relate to one another directly affects the quality of child care and sets an example for children, adults in a child-care setting work to resolve issues and problems among themselves cooperatively and respectfully. They also work together to educate the community at large about the needs of young children. The child care provider should develop relationships with other child care professionals and establish a network for information and support.

Examples

For example, the competent Candidate working with preschool children:

- ☐ Enjoys working with young children in a group setting and demonstrates a positive attitude in her/his role.

- ☐ Understands the philosophy of the program and can describe its goals and objectives to others.

- ☐ Continues to gain knowledge of physical, cognitive, language, emotional, and social development as a basis for planning program goals.

- ☐ Keeps all personal information about children and families confidential.

☐ Continually evaluates own performance to identify needs for professional growth.

☐ Participates in peer evaluation and is able to accept comments and criticism from colleagues, supervisors, and parents in a constructive way.

☐ Takes advantage of opportunities for professional and personal development by joining appropriate professional organizations and attending meetings, courses, and conferences.

☐ Keeps informed about child care practices, research, legislation, and other developments in early childhood education.

☐ Candidate keeps abreast of current regulatory, legislative and workforce issues and knows how they affect the welfare of young children and families.

☐ Seeks information relevant to the needs of the children s/he is serving — for example, information on school readiness, bilingual development, and special needs — from professional magazines, community colleges, community services, other caregivers, and community members.

☐ Recognizes that caregiver fatigue, low morale, and lack of work satisfaction decrease effectiveness and finds ways to meet her/his own needs and maintain energy and enthusiasm.

☐ Works cooperatively with other staff members, accepts supervision, and helps promote a positive atmosphere in the center.

☐ Learns about new laws and regulations affecting center care, children, and families.

☐ Advocates for high quality services and rights for children and families.

☐ Works with other professionals and parents to develop effective strategies to communicate to decision makers the needs of the children and families.

☐ Develops the ability to state needs for additional resources for individual children or some aspect of the program.

☐ Is aware that some of the typical developmental characteristics of children *(for example, crying, messiness, dependency, willfulness, negative behavior, curiosity about genital differences)* often make adults uncomfortable. The caregiver can acknowledge these feelings in her/himself, co-workers, and parents while minimizing negative reactions toward children.

☐ Seeks information about sexual abuse and child abuse and neglect, keeps up-to-date on laws and policies concerning reporting and treatment of abuse, and learns effective ways of working with affected children and families.

☐ Is familiar with the NAEYC Code of Ethical Conduct.

☐ Engages in ongoing professional development.

Bilingual Specialization

In addition, the competent Candidate working towards a bilingual specialization, for example:

☐ Demonstrates ability to understand, speak, read, and write in both languages and uses these skills in all aspects of the program.

☐ Increases knowledge about bilingual education by reading, attending workshops, and consulting professionals.

☐ Maintains and works to increase fluency in her/his second language.

☐ Consistently provides opportunities for all children to acquire a second language.

☐ Promotes the effective functioning of the bilingual program by attempting to clarify issues relating to bilingualism and multiculturalism.

Principles for Dual Language Learners

Young children whose home language is not English are participants in many early childhood centers and family child care homes. These children are referred to as ***dual language learners*** because they are either learning two languages simultaneously or adding a new (second) language to their primary (home) language. The following developmental principles and accompanying practice examples are presented separately to emphasize that they apply to all Competency Standards and Functional Areas. These principles and examples provide important guidance to help teachers work competently with dual language learners.

Developmental Context

Infants and toddlers exposed to two languages at home or in an early childhood program have the opportunity to develop basic language ability in two languages simultaneously (**simultaneous dual-language acquisition**). However, when young children (aged 3, 4 and 5 years) whose families' primary language is not English begin participating in a preschool or family child care home, they have most likely established basic language ability in their home language. For these children this opportunity for second language acquisition is referred to as **sequential dual-language acquisition**. Early childhood programs can also offer opportunities for second language acquisition to children whose home language is English. However, the following developmental principles and examples focus on young English language learners in preschool programs.

The research literature on second language acquisition identifies the following four developmental stages (Tabors, 2008; Espinosa , 2010).

1. **Home language use.** Young children who have established basic oral communication ability in their home language naturally enter the preschool setting using their familiar home language. The degree to which these children experience being understood by others depends on whether any of the adults or children speak their home language.

2. **Nonverbal/observational period.** When young children speaking their home language are frequently not understood, they begin speaking less and turn their attention to observing, listening, and using nonverbal means of communication. This developmental stage is very important as the child is actively learning the sounds, words, and rules of the new language. These children are building their receptive understanding of their new language — connecting the sounds and words

to people, objects, and experiences. There can be wide variance in the amount of time any child operates at this stage of development.

3. **Telegraphic and formulaic speech**. Children begin trying out their new language, using simple words or phrases to express thoughts, requests, and directions. Although the child may not know the specific meaning of these words and phrases, dual language learners are focused on results — do they work for social interactions or achieve the desired response from an adult. This form of early language production also enables these children to begin participating in group singing or reciting rhymes.

4. **Productive language**. Dual language learners begin building their own original sentences using words and phrases they have been hearing and practicing. This is a gradual phase as children test what works and experiment with applying grammar rules of their new language. Each child's productive language is closely related to their expansion of receptive language.

Adults who successfully work with young dual language learners understand that although each of the above developmental stages build on each other, beginning to use productive language does not replace earlier phases in particular situations. In some circumstances a child will revert to nonverbal observation and listening. Effective teachers are also sensitive to numerous factors that influence the rate and proficiency of each child's acquisition of a new language — amount and quality of exposure to English; age and culture; motivation and interest in new language; personality; and degree of accepting relationships that support trying new language (Tabors, 2008). Understanding that there will be individual differences between children is essential to providing the best possible support for dual language development.

An extremely important component of good early childhood programs and family child care homes is providing a learning environment that is supportive of the language development of all children. For dual language learners this means providing age appropriate, individually appropriate, and culturally appropriate experiences that help children begin to understand and use the English language while simultaneously developing their primary (home) language. This includes encouraging parents to provide their children with a strong foundation in their home language.

When a child's second language (typically English) is used predominantly by the surrounding society, home language development and maintenance may become more difficult. Nevertheless, research shows that second language learners do best in school when they have a strong grounding in their home language (Espinosa, 2010; Oiler & Eilers,

2002; Slavin & Cheung, 2005).The loss of the first language can be detrimental not only for personal, familial, religious, and cultural reasons, but it can also negatively impact children's progress in school. Teachers can help families value and support their child to continue developing the home language while also learning a second language.

Practice – *Examples*

The competent Candidate working with dual language learners is **knowledgeable about and respectful of child's family, culture, and home language**.

- Seeks information about language spoken at home and child's proficiency in the home language.

- Expresses interest in, and respects, families' priorities related to their child including attitude toward maintaining home language and acquiring English.

- Makes effort to learn about child's home culture and beliefs as well as the people, pets, activities and objects that are familiar and important to the child. Incorporates appropriate artifacts and pictures into the center to help introduce English words and phrases for things already familiar to the preschooler.

- Maintains communication with families and/or child's primary caregiver to track the child's developmental gains in the home language.

- Is knowledgeable about and respectful of child's family.

- Asks parents for a few words in the home language that can be used to welcome the child in the classroom (*e.g., with parents' permission makes a tape recording of these words to use in the classroom to comfort their child and to help other children hear the sounds of the child's home language*).

The competent Candidate working with dual language learners **establishes responsive and accepting relationships** *to help children feel confident to engage in receptive and verbal communication in either language — home language or new language:*

- Builds positive, warm, nurturing relationships with dual language learners so that they feel safe and less anxious. Speaks English in ways that help dual language learners understand: uses simple sentences, repeats what is said, uses gestures and facial expressions, points to objects, uses everyday vocabulary.

- Speaks English clearly and slowly but not loudly, simplifying language when needed as you would for a younger child who is just learning their first language so the child more easily hears and learns individual words and phrases.

- Uses repetition so child hears the same word or phrase multiple times and consistently paired with the same object, person, or action.

- Gradually complicates own language so dual language learners continue to make progress in vocabulary development.

- Individualizes interactions that help each child gain trust in new people and environment.

- Is responsive and encouraging when child attempts verbal communication in either language — home language or new language.

- Provides verbal respectful response in the language the child is attempting to speak *(if possible)*.

- Recognizes when child mouths words or says words to self and encourages these attempts.

- Provides social support for dual language learners — regular contact with other children or adults who speak their language to help support their identity and help them make sense of what's going on.

- Provides lots of time and opportunities for children to play and talk among themselves.

- Encourages interactions between dual-language learners and English-speaking children by modeling initiations *(e.g., Candidate says to a child "Ask Lili, may I play with you?")*.

- Pairs an English language learner with an outgoing English-speaking child for certain periods during the day, so that the English-speaking child may help to integrate the English language learner into classroom activities.

The competent Candidate working with dual language learners provides **numerous appropriate experiences to help children gain receptive understanding** *of the new language — specifically, to hear the sounds of the new language and connect them to people, objects and experiences.*

- Uses predictable, comfortable classroom routines so dual language learners know what to expect and uses consistent language when referring to activities *(clean up time)* and objects *(cubby, house area, block area, monkey bars, etc.)* throughout the day in the classroom and outdoors.

- Provides pictures to accompany the daily schedule, classroom rules, and other print in the classroom to help children know the expectations even though they may not yet understand the language.

- Consistently accompanies verbal communications with gestures, actions, visual aids, or directed gaze to help child interpret directions *(e.g. models washing hands while saying "Let's wash your hands")* or descriptions of actions *(e.g. "Here is your jacket, or book, or snack")*.

- Helps children link English vocabulary to firsthand experiences with pictures, concrete objects and real-life events. For the most part, talks about the here and now, until children become more proficient in English.

- Selects books, songs, poems with repetitive language and repeats them frequently. Uses music and physical actions to help children learn new phrases and sentences *("Head, shoulders, knees, and toes")*.

- Reads books, if possible in child's primary language prior to reading the book in English, always pointing to pictures associated with words and phrases.

- Provides small group reading times using concept books or predictable texts *(like Brown Bear, Brown Bear)* with simplified vocabulary where children can clearly see the pictures and follow along. Reads the same book repeatedly, as long as children are enjoying it, to build comprehension. Reads *(or provides audiotapes)* in the child's home language.

- Describes in simple words and phrases the actions of the child *(e.g., "You are rolling the ball")* or actions of other children he/she is observing *(e.g., "Molly is rocking the doll")*.

- Places words at the end of the sentence to give emphasis to those words *(e.g. "You have red shoes. Billy has black shoes")*.

- Keeps alert to a dual language learner's use of non-verbal communication, such as pointing silently to a milk carton. Supplies the words in English for what the child is trying to convey *(e.g., "would you like more milk? Sure, I will be glad to give you more milk.")*

- Intentionally introduces new vocabulary words and uses the words throughout the day.

The competent Candidate working with dual language learners provides **experiences to encourage and help children practice sounds and words of the new language** *taking into account the stages and patterns of home language and English acquisition as well as information about each child's progress in cognitive, social-emotional, and physical development.*

- Encourages child to repeat words as she or he demonstrates what objects or pictures they refer to.

- Gives child lots of time to think about what they want to say and waits to offer options of the word or phrase they are searching for when the child appears to wish for help.

- Asks young learners of the second language close-ended questions and offers some options for their response (*e.g., "Do you want the doll or do you want the clown?"*).

- Pauses and lets the child fill in the next word when reading books.

- Provides opportunities to be able to answer in chorus with all the children.

- Helps children go from non-verbal responses to more expressive responses (e.g., child looks at his shirt with spilled juice and looks at the Candidate; Candidate responds "Do you need me to change your shirt?" Child: "change shirt." Candidate: "That is right, I will be glad to change your shirt.")

- Is able to expand child's vocabulary (*e.g., child says "yucky." Candidate responds "Yes, the floor is really dirty, yucky"*).

- Notices words or phrases the child says (*"me", "like", "more"*) and helps child build from those words or phrases (*Candidate says "I like you!" "You want more"*).

- Provides experiences for the child to play with the sounds: lullabies, repetitive singing and games, poems that repeat words.

- Understands that code switching or language mixing are typical and natural aspects of second language acquisition and enhances communication, and **does not impose rigid rules about language** (*e.g., child says "me asustado del doggie." Candidate responds: "Oh, I know — you are afraid of dogs"*).

- Models correct English version of a phrase used by a dual language learner (*e.g., if a child says "I goed to park," the Candidate responds: "You went to the park? Who went with you?"*)

- Engages child in conversations of topics that are interesting and important to him/her and that are part of their life experiences.

- Provides English language learners opportunities for one-on-one interaction with another child or adult where they may be more comfortable trying out English. But also plans for English language learners to have small group experiences — sometimes with children who are English language learners and other times with mixed groups of English speaking and English language learning children because each context offers different growth opportunities.

- Helps children acquire skills, knowledge, and attitudes such as book knowledge and appreciation, print awareness, letter knowledge, and phonological awareness in their home language. Once acquired, these skills will transfer as children become proficient in English.

- Includes environmental print *(signs, labels, books, magazines, newspapers and other text)* in English and the child's home language.

References:

Espinosa, L. (2010). *Getting it right for young children from diverse backgrounds: Applying research to improve practice.* Upper Saddle River, NJ: Pearson.

Oller, K. D., & Eilers, R. E. (Eds.). (2002). *Language and literacy in bilingual children.* New York: Multi-Lingual Matters.

Slavin, R. E., & Cheung, A. (2005). A synthesis of research on language of reading instruction for English language learners. *Review of Educational Research,* 75 (2), 247-281.

Tabors, P.O. 2008. *One child, two languages: A guide for early childhood educators of children learning English as a second language (2nd ed.).* Baltimore: Paul H. Brookes Publishing, Co.

PART IV
Appendices

Appendix A: History of the Child Development Associate Program

The Child Development Associate concept grew out of concern in the late 1960's with the rapid expansion of public and private child care programs serving children five years old and younger. During the decade of the 1960's, hundreds of Head Start centers had been established across the country to serve economically disadvantaged preschoolers, and the number of licensed child care centers had tripled, as many mothers returned to work. Although the number of children in care increased yearly, there was no concerted effort to monitor the quality of care children received. At the same time, major research studies stressed the importance of early childhood care to children's later development.

In 1970, the Administration on Children, Youth, and Families *(ACYF)*, of the Department of Health, Education and Welfare announced its commitment to improve the quality of child care by focusing on the competence of child care staff. In 1971, the agency convened a group of leaders in the early childhood/child development field to examine the idea of establishing professional recognition for competent child care personnel. The ACYF task force envisioned a nationally supported effort to:

- identify basic competencies *(or skills)* needed by staff to provide competent care;

- provide training for caregivers in these competencies; and

- evaluate the work of caregivers on the basis of these national standards and recognize them with a national "credential" or award.

In 1972, several early childhood education/child development associations established a nonprofit consortium to develop and carry out a system for evaluating and credentialing child care workers on the basis of the competencies outlined by the federal task force. The Child Development Associate *(CDA)* Consortium refined the original competencies, developed a more detailed description of the skills needed to deliver quality care, and designed a system for assessing child care workers on the job.

Within two years, the organization had developed an assessment system for performance-based evaluation of child care workers serving 3- to 5-year-olds in center-based programs, based on six Competency Standards. A 1974 field test was successful, and the assessment system was implemented the next year. The first CDA Credentials were awarded in July 1975. In 1979, bilingual Competency Standards and assessment requirements were added to the system so that CDA Candidates working in bilingual programs *(Spanish/English)* could demonstrate their special competence.

The CDA Consortium administered the program from its inception until 1979. The Child Development Associate National Credentialing Program *(CDANCP)*, administered by Bank Street College of Education in New York under a grant from the Department of Health and Human Services, implemented CDA assessments until the Spring of 1985. During its tenure, the CDANCP undertook a major research project to investigate expansion of the CDA assessment system to caregivers in home visitor and family child care programs, as well as to center caregivers working with infants and toddlers and disabled children. Field testing of requirements and competencies in the home visitor, family child care, and infant/toddler center-based programs was successful, and CDA assessment was made available to caregivers working in these settings between 1983 and 1985.

In Spring of 1985, the National Association for the Education of Young Children *(NAEYC)* entered into a 42-month cooperative agreement with the Administration for Children, Youth and Families *(ACYF)* and assumed responsibility for management of the CDA Program. NAEYC set up a separate nonprofit corporation entitled, "The Council for Early Childhood Professional Recognition" (the *Council*), to serve as the national CDA body to administer the CDA Program. The Council took full responsibility on September 1, 1985.

Under the auspices of the Council, three years of nationwide study and review were conducted in the interest of making the CDA program more accessible, affordable and credible. The procedures for assessment were revised and national standards for the delivery of CDA training were established.

CDA Training

The training component of the CDA effort has been funded and administered separately from assessment and credentialing responsibilities since the beginning of the project. In 1973, ACYF funded 13 pilot training programs to develop performance-based training designed to help caregivers master the CDA competencies. At the same time, Head Start Supplementary Training was converted to a CDA orientation, with colleges and universities across the country participating in this effort.

Today, field-based CDA training is conducted by child care programs, Head Start centers, and many colleges and universities. The Council also administers a one-year program: the CDA Professional Preparation Program (*CDA P$_3$*).

Individuals can become CDAs by participating in a variety of training experiences for early childhood staff in their local community. Once trained, they can apply to the Council for assessment according to national standards and procedures.

Appendix B: Glossary of CDA Terms

Advisor. A professional in early childhood education who observes the Candidate at work and completes the CDA Assessment Observation Instrument.

Application *(or **Direct Assessment Application Form**)*. A form that notifies the Council that a CDA Candidate is ready for assessment. After the Candidate and Advisor have completed their information collection responsibilities, the Candidate fills out all parts of the application form. Both the Candidate and Advisor will sign it and mail it to the Council. After receiving the application form, the Council assigns a Council Representative, who will make a Verification Visit.

Assessment System. The process by which a caregiver's competence is evaluated by the Council. The **CDA Assessment System** includes these stages: (1) Inquiry; (2) Collection of Documentation; (3) Application; (4) Verification Visit; (5) Credential Award; and (6) Credential Renewal.

Bilingual Program. A Bilingual program is one which has specific goals for achieving bilingual development in children; where two languages are consistently used in daily activities; and where parents are helped to understand the goals and to support children's bilingual development.

Candidate. An individual who has applied for CDA assessment and who has met all eligibility requirements. A CDA Candidate coordinates the information collection responsibility of the Advisor and ensures that parent/opinion questionnaires have been distributed and collected. The Candidate also participates in the Verification Visit with the Council Representative.

CDA. Child Development Associate. An individual who has successfully completed a CDA assessment and who has been awarded the CDA Credential. A CDA is a person who is able to meet the specific needs of children and who, with parents and other adults, works to nurture children's physical, social, emotional, and intellectual growth in a child development framework. The CDA conducts her/himself in an ethical manner. The CDA has demonstrated competence in the CDA Competency Goals through her/his work in a center-based, home visitor, or family child care program. A person who has demonstrated bilingual competence in a bilingual child care program is a CDA with a bilingual specialization.

CDA Assessment Observation Instrument. The official form used by Advisors to record observations of the Candidate in the 13 Functional Areas.

CDA Consortium. The **CDA Consortium** was established in 1972 as an organization of national professional associations concerned with ensuring the competence of staff in child development programs. The Consortium developed the original CDA Competency Standards and the system for assessing individuals working in center-based programs with 3- to 5-year-olds. The organization administered CDA assessments from 1975 to 1979. The CDA Consortium is no longer operating.

CDA Training. Programs that guide, teach, and support individuals interested in a CDA assessment offered by child care programs, colleges, and universities. The CDA assessment system requires educational experiences in early childhood/child development, but these do not have to be **CDA training** experiences. Whether or not an individual is enrolled in CDA training does not affect eligibility for an assessment.

Center-Based. One of the settings a Candidate may choose for CDA assessment. A **center-based** setting for CDA assessment is defined as a "state-approved child development center." When a Candidate chooses to be assessed in a center-based setting, s/he uses the Competency Standards, eligibility requirements, and information collection requirements designed for that setting.

Clock Hour. 60 minutes.

Code of Ethical Conduct. Standards of ethical behavior developed for the early childhood profession by the National Association for the Education of Young Children.

Cognitive. Cognitive development is the growth of understanding and knowledge. It is sometimes described as *intellectual development*.

Competence. Skill or ability to do something well.

Competency Goals. General statements of competence that a caregiver should work towards. There are **six CDA Competency Goals**:

       I. to establish and maintain a safe, healthy learning environment;

       II. to advance physical and intellectual competence;

       III. to support social and emotional development and to provide positive guidance;

       IV. to establish positive and productive relationships with families;

       V. to ensure a well-run, purposeful program responsive to participant needs; and

       VI. to maintain a commitment to professionalism

Competency Standards. Criteria that define the goals and skills that a competent child care provider or home visitor should demonstrate in working with young children. The **Competency Standards** consists of six Goals, 13 Functional Areas, and examples of competent behavior. They were developed and validated by the early childhood profession and approved by the CDA Consortium.

Conflict of Interest. A relationship that may interfere with an Advisor's ability to be objective in assessing a Candidate. The Advisor:

1. Must not be working as co-teacher with the Candidate on a daily basis in the room or group where the Candidate will be observed.

2. Must not be a relative of a child in the Candidate's care at any time between information collection and the Verification Visit.

3. Must not be related by blood or marriage, or other legal relationship to the Candidate.

Council Representative. A professional in early childhood education, trained and endorsed by the Council to conduct a Verification Visit for a CDA Candidate.

Credential. A written document from an authorizing body showing that a person has met certain standards. The CDA Credential is awarded by the Council to caregivers who have demonstrated competence in the CDA Competency Standards during the CDA assessment process.

Developmental Context. The CDA Competency Standards include a developmental context for each of the 13 Functional Areas. It includes a brief summary of children's development and a context for a caregiver's work with children at the different stages of development.

Direct Assessment Application Form. See Application.

Dual language learners. Children who are learning two languages simultaneously or adding a new (second) language to their primary (home) language.

Early Childhood Studies Review. The CDA written examination.

Eligibility Requirements. Requirements that individuals must meet in order to participate in the CDA Assessment process. **Eligibility requirements for the Advisor and Council Rep are listed respectively in Appendix C and D of this book.**

Endorsement. An applicant for CDA assessment in a center-based setting must choose one endorsement for assessment. The age of the children the Candidate works with determines whether the endorsement is preschool *(3 through 5 years)* or infant/toddler *(birth to age 36 months)*. Family child care providers and home visitors are assessed on their work with the families and children in their care who may range in age from birth through five years.

Expansion. Activities carried out to make the CDA Credential available to groups of child care workers not presently eligible. Between 1980 and 1985, expansion work was completed on standards and assessment systems for home visitors, caregivers working with infants and toddlers, and family child care providers.

Family Child Care. One of the settings a Candidate may choose for CDA assessment. A family child care setting for CDA assessment is defined as a family child care home that meets at least the minimum level of applicable state and local regulations, where a Candidate can be observed working as a primary caregiver with at least two children five years old or younger who are not related to the Candidate by blood or marriage or other legal relationship.

Formal Education. Child care training/preparation for work with children and families. A CDA Applicant must have completed 120 clock hours of such preparation. The CDA Candidate must have had comprehensive instruction in early childhood education/child development in eight subject areas.

Functional Area. A category of responsibility that defines a caregiver's role in relation to children. The six CDA Competency Goals are divided in 13 **Functional Areas** defined by the following key words: Safe, Healthy, Learning Environment, Physical, Cognitive, Communication, Creative, Self, Social, Guidance, Families, Program Management, and Professionalism. Each Functional Area is defined by a sentence that summarizes competent caregiver behavior.

Home Visitor. One of the settings a Candidate may choose for CDA assessment. A home visitor setting is defined as an established program of home visits to families to work with children five years old or younger and to support parents in meeting the needs of their young children. In this setting, regular home visits are the primary method of program delivery. When a Candidate chooses to be assessed in a home visitor setting, s/he uses the Competency Standards, eligibility requirements, and information collection responsibilities designed for that setting.

Oral Interview. A situation-based assessment of the Candidate's knowledge of the 13 Functional Areas.

Parent Questionnaires. The Candidate distributes a Parent Questionnaire to each family that has a child in her/his group or to each family the Candidate visits. The questionnaires give parents an opportunity to describe and evaluate the Candidates' work from their point of view.

Professional Resource File. A collection of materials early childhood professionals use in their work with young children and families. It is divided into three parts: (1) Autobiography; (2) Statements of Competence; and (3) Resource Collection.

Renewal. The process of revalidating a CDA Credential when it expires. The CDA Credential is valid for three years from the date of award. At the end of that period, a CDA can apply for renewal of the Credential. When renewal is granted, the Credential becomes valid for an additional five years.

Setting. The type of child care program in which a CDA Candidate's performance is evaluated. An applicant for a CDA assessment chooses one of the following settings: center-based program, family child care program, or home visitor program. The CDA Competency Standards, eligibility requirements, and information collection responsibilities are different for each setting.

Specialization. An applicant for CDA assessment has an option to be assessed for a bilingual specialization. The applicant must work in a program where the two languages and cultures are used consistently with adults and children. The applicant must also be able to speak, read, and write both Spanish and English.

Supplemental Observation Form. Documentation of Candidate interacting with children in the age range not represented during the initial observation. Supplemental observations are applicable only to Infant/Toddler Candidates.

Trainer. A child development/child care specialist who teaches classes, conducts workshops, models activities with children and families, or works with caregivers individually to improve their skills. Many child care programs have staff or consultants who work as CDA trainers. Sometimes a trainer may become a Candidate's CDA Advisor. However, a Candidate is not required to choose a CDA trainer as the CDA Advisor.

Waiver(s). Certain eligibility information collection requirements for Candidates and Advisors may be suspended by the Council. Each request must be submitted on the Waiver Request Form located at the end of Part II of this manual.

Appendix C: Advisor Eligibility Requirements

The Advisor must meet the following eligibility requirements and provide verification on the Candidate's Application Form:

Personal

- Affirm her/his ability to relate to people of various racial, ethnic, and socio-economic backgrounds.

- Be knowledgeable about local, state, and national requirements, standards, and guidelines for child care programs serving children aged birth through 5 years.

- Be familiar with the center where the Candidate will be observed and the needs of families and children in the community.

Education and Experience

The Advisor must meet all of the requirements in one of the three combinations of education and experience outlined in sections 1, 2, or 3 below:

Section 1

- B.A., B.S., or advanced degree in early childhood education/child development, home economics/child development, from an accredited college or university. Must include 12 semester hours covering children aged birth through 5 years.

- Two years of experience in a child care setting serving children aged 3 through 5 years, including:

  - **One year** working directly with children as a caregiver, teacher, child life worker, social worker, or similar role; and

  - **One year** of responsibility for the professional growth of another adult.

Section 2

- Associate-level *(two-year)* degree in early childhood education/child development, home economics/child development, from an accredited college or university. Must include 12 semester hours covering children aged birth through 5 years.

- Four years of experience in a child care setting in a program serving children aged 3 through 5 years, including:

    - **Two years** of experience working directly with children as a caregiver, teacher, child life worker, social worker, or similar role; and

    - **Two years** of responsibility for the professional growth of another adult.

Section 3

- An active CDA Credential

- Twelve semester hours of study in early childhood education or child development at an accredited college or university covering children aged birth through 5 years.

- Six years of experience in a child care setting serving children aged 3 through 5 years, including:

    - **Four years** working directly with children as a caregiver, teacher, child life worker, social worker, or similar role; and

    - **Two years** of responsibility for the professional growth of another adult.

Bilingual Specialization

In addition to meeting the requirements listed in sections 1, 2, or 3, an Advisor for Bilingual Specialization Assessment must meet the following requirements:

- Be able to speak, read, and write English and the other language well enough to understand and be understood by both children and adults.

- Have direct experience with bilingual early childhood programs and with non-English-speaking populations.

Conflict of Interest

To promote objectivity and credibility, an individual serving as an Advisor:

1. Must not be working as co-teacher with the Candidate on a daily basis in the same room or group.

2. Must not be the relative of a child in the Candidate's care at any time during the assessment process.

3. Must not be related by blood or marriage or other legal relationship to the Candidate.

Waivers

The Council will consider waiving certain education and training requirements if an individual provides a written explanation and documentation of alternative formal and informal training related to early childhood education/child development and experience in early childhood teacher preparation.

Waiver petitions must be documented on the Waiver Request Form provided on page 35.

Appendix D: Council Representative Eligibility Requirements

To conduct assessments as a Council Representative, an individual must meet the following criteria:

PERSONAL

- Affirm her/his ability to relate to people of various racial, ethnic, and socioeconomic backgrounds.

- Be knowledgeable about local, state, and national requirements, standards, and guidelines for child care programs serving children aged birth through 5 years.

- Be familiar with the center where the Candidate will be observed and the needs of families and children in the community.

EDUCATIONAL BACKGROUND

Hold a Baccalaureate or Associate degree from an accredited college or university in one of the following disciplines:

- **Early Childhood Education/Child Development**
- **Elementary Education/Early Childhood Education**
- **Home Economics/Child Development**

The degree must include, at minimum, **18 semester or 24 quarter hours of coursework in Early Childhood Education/Child Development,** studying children aged from birth to 5 years of age.

PRACTICAL EXPERIENCE

Option A.

For those with a BACCALAUREATE DEGREE, **TWO YEARS** in a child care setting serving children from birth to 5 years of age, to include: **one year** working directly with children as a caregiver, teacher, child life worker, social worker, or similar role, **AND one year** facilitating the professional growth of at least one other adult.

Option B.

For those with an ASSOCIATE DEGREE, **FOUR YEARS** in a child care setting serving children from birth to 5 years of age, to include: **two years** working directly with children as a caregiver, teacher, child life worker, social worker, or similar role, **AND two years** facilitating the professional growth of at least one other adult.

WAIVERS

A variety of experiences, such as teaching college coursework, may be submitted to document expertise in Early Childhood Education/Child Development. All such substitutions should be submitted in writing for Council approval.